2 0 JUN 2022

NUMERACY AND BEYOND

Please return
- if

R

D0279925

NUMERACY AND BEYOND

Applying mathematics in the primary school

Martin Hughes,
Charles Desforges and
Christine Mitchell
with Clive Carré

Open University Press
Buckingham · Philadelphia

Open University Press
Celtic Court
22 Ballmoor
Buckingham
MK18 1XW

e-mail: enquiries@openup.co.uk
world wide web: http://www.openup.co.uk

and
325 Chestnut Street
Philadelphia, PA 19106, USA

First Published 2000

A catalogue record of this book is available from the British Library

ISBN   0 335 20129 6 (pb)   0 335 20130 X (hb)

Library of Congress Cataloging-in-Publication Data
Hughes, Martin, 1949 May 15
    Numeracy and beyond : applying mathematics in the primary school / Martin Hughes, Charles Desforges, and Christine Mitchell with Clive Carré.
        p. cm.
    Includes bibliographical references and index.
    ISBN 0-335-20130-X (hb)
    ISBN 0-335-20129-6 (pb)
    1. Mathematics – Study and teaching (Primary) – Great Britain.
2. Mathematics – Study and teaching (Primary) – Japan. I. Desforges, Charles.
II. Mitchell, Christine. III. Title.
    QA135.5.H844 2000   99-32466
    372.7'2'0'41–dc21   CIP

Typeset by Type Study, Scarborough
Printed in Great Britain by St Edmundsbury Press Ltd, Bury St Edmunds, Suffolk

Contents

Introduction

> I think using and applying is very hard work because in my view it is demanding the children to make connections themselves. They are actively engaging with the current problem with their existing knowledge and trying to make the two meet, and I think that is hard work.
>
> (Year 5 teacher)

This book is about the problem of application in mathematics. By this we mean the fact that people frequently have difficulty applying mathematical knowledge acquired in one context to problems posed in another. As the above comment suggests, applying mathematical knowledge in this way can often be 'hard work' for children – and for adults too. We hope that as a result of this book ways can be found for making application somewhat easier.

Numeracy and Beyond has been written at a time of intense international concern about standards of mathematical attainment in schools. In England and Wales, this has focused on a concern with 'numeracy'. The National Numeracy Strategy, in place since 1998, is aimed at raising standards of numeracy in young people. The specific objective of the strategy is to meet the target set in 1997 by the incoming Labour Government: by the year 2002 at least 75 per cent of 11-year-olds will reach the level in mathematics appropriate for their age. As a result of the National Numeracy Strategy widespread changes have been made to the way mathematics is taught in primary schools in England and Wales, based around the daily mathematics lesson or 'numeracy hour'.

We believe that application is at the heart of numeracy. At all levels of learning mathematics pupils need to use and build on what they already know in order to progress further. But they also need to learn how to use their existing knowledge when they are confronted by new problems in novel contexts. There is little point in pupils being 'numerate' if they cannot apply what they know.

Yet despite the importance of application in mathematics, its problematic nature is frequently unrecognized. If pupils fail to apply what they know, they are often blamed for being 'stupid', or their teachers are blamed for 'poor teaching'. We would suggest instead a third explanation; the problem of application is more complex, deeply rooted and resistant to solution than many people realize. The problem of application, in short, is a problem that is poorly understood.

Our overall aim in this book is to increase understanding of the problem of application in mathematics. We do so by examining the issue from a number of different perspectives.

We start in Chapter 1 by looking at the nature and extent of the problem, and at the way it has been conceptualized within different theories of learning. Chapter 2 looks at how application has been addressed within the mathematics curriculum in England and Wales, and how it is currently being treated within the National Numeracy Strategy. In Chapters 3, 4 and 5 we present examples of what a group of primary teachers did and said as they attempted to develop ways of 'teaching for application'. These examples are not presented as models of 'best practice'; rather, they suggest some possible ways forward for teachers wanting to develop their own practice, as well as raising some of the issues and dilemmas underlying different approaches to application. Chapter 6 presents some examples of practice from primary school teachers in Japan. These Japanese teachers were using a 'whole class teaching' approach that closely resembles that recommended in the National Numeracy Strategy, and their methods are therefore of considerable relevance for teachers attempting to implement the strategy in this country. Finally, Chapter 7 brings together what we have learned from these different perspectives, and looks at the issues that they raise.

Numeracy and Beyond is intended for anyone who is concerned about the problem of application and who wants to understand it further. We hope that it will be read by: student and practising teachers as they attempt to develop their teaching within the National Numeracy Strategy; by LEA advisors and numeracy consultants, who have pivotal roles within the strategy; and by mathematics educators and educational researchers. We have therefore attempted to write in a way that is clear and accessible to these different groups.

The teachers whose practice is described in Chapters 3, 4 and 5 were part of a project, 'Using and Applying Mathematics in the Primary School', funded by the Nuffield Foundation. This project grew out of an informal inquiry into primary mathematics, which was set up by Anthony Tomei of the Nuffield Foundation. As part of this inquiry, we organized seminars, established contact with mathematics educators in this country and abroad, and visited Japan. We would like to thank the Nuffield Foundation and all those involved in the inquiry – and particularly Anthony Tomei, Margaret Brown and Ruth Merttens – for supporting our project and helping us develop our thinking. We would also like to thank Janet Ainley, Margaret Brown, Pamela Greenhough, Sandra Pendlington and Bill Rawson for their helpful comments on an earlier draft, and Shona Mullen, our editor at Open University Press, for her support and patience as deadlines came and went. Finally, we would like to thank the many teachers and children in English primary schools who took part in the project, and the teachers and mathematics educators in Japan, and particularly Hiroshi Agata, Atsuhiro Fukuchi and Tadao Nakahara, who made our visit there so enlightening. At the same time, we should make it clear that all names used in the book for teachers and children (both English and Japanese) are pseudonyms.

The problem of application

We attend school in order to learn a body of knowledge and skills that we might use in all aspects of our lives. For example, when we learn to read it is not so that we might merely read school books. We learn to read so that we may read for pleasure, for information and for further learning in all aspects of our lives, in and out of school, and beyond into our professional and domestic lives.

The business of application is relevant to all curriculum subjects. As we shall see in this chapter, it is a complex and difficult matter, particularly with regard to mathematics. For the purposes of illustration, we start our discussion with the somewhat easier and more familiar case of reading.

Applying knowledge of reading

For most of us, once we have learned to read our infant school books, the skill of reading seems to flow almost effortlessly into other books, magazines, posters, signs and print of all kinds. Almost effortlessly. Occasionally we cannot make sense of some text. We pause, perhaps, to look up a new word, or to try to make sense of familiar words in new contexts. Such delays in the sense making process of reading become less frequent as we become more experienced. The general feeling of being able to read seems to flow more and more easily to the whole range of text in print. Even though almost everything we read is new, never before seen in quite that way, we seem to have little difficulty in using our knowledge of reading to make sense of new texts. We apply our basic knowledge and skills of reading to new settings.

Authors and designers may change the print size, the format of type or the layout of text on the page. They may experiment with colour and with combinations of words and other signs and symbols. The good reader, rather than being defeated by such antics, is often intrigued. What do you make, for example, of the following?

Wants pawn term, dare worsted ladle gull
hoe lift wetter murder inner ladle cordage
honor itch offer lodge, dock florist.
Disc ladle gull orphan worry ladle cluck
wetter putty ladle rat hut,
end fur disc raisin pimple colder
ladle rat rotten hut

Every word in the above is a legitimate English word but clearly it does not mean what it says. If you have not already made sense of it, read the text again as the start of a traditional and well known children's story. Now you see a playful introduction to Little Red Riding Hood.

You have applied your knowledge of reading to a new experience of reading. You have solved a problem. In doing so you have obviously used a lot more knowledge than that involved in merely voicing individual words. You have brought to bear your knowledge of children's stories and made the association between particular words and a much more general understanding of the story of Little Red Riding Hood. With this understanding in mind you will now be able to read the part of the story where Little Red Riding Hood meets the wolf:

'Wail, wail, wail,' set disc wicket woof,
'evanescent ladle rat rotten hut!
Wares or putty ladle gull goring
wizard ladle backing?'

'Armor goring tumor groin murder's',
reprisal ladle gull.
'Grammars seeking bet.'

(Adams 1990: 223)

Many people take pleasure out of making sense of this sort of thing, just as they take pleasure and profit in making sense out of complex words, challenging instruction books or higher level text and reference books. There are some people, of course, who do not find pleasure in reading, or who find it hard to progress beyond – or even achieve – basic levels of understanding. Nevertheless, for most readers, the skill of applying reading skills across a wide range of contexts is taken for granted. It seems unremarkable.

There are many other cases where we learn something in a particular setting and transfer our learning readily to other contexts. For example, the first time we see someone using a hammer to knock a nail into a piece of wood the circumstances are very particular. The hammer is a certain type, size and colour. The nail is a particular material, copper say, or iron, and the wood is of a particular type in a specific place and orientation. Most of us, however, are able to generalize from our informal lesson in hammering. We are able, without further tuition, to use hammers of all kinds to beat pointed objects of many varieties into materials of any type and in any position. Where a proper hammer is not to hand we invent substitutes. Any hard object that can be handled like a hammer is brought to bear on the job. Shoes are particularly available hammer surrogates. All this is unremarkable, and taken for granted.

We can, as we have above, describe our achievements in terms of the transfer of learning or the application of knowledge and skills. We might say that we transfer what we know from one situation or setting to another situation. Or we might say that we apply what we have learned in one context to a novel problem in another context. The two contexts might be quite similar or very different. The differences between one book and the next in a Year 1 reading scheme are very slight. The typeface, layout, colour, characters and almost all the vocabulary are deliberately kept the same. Still, a certain amount of application is needed to make sense of the few new words in the many new sentences. The situation in which there is little difference between the two contexts is said to require *near transfer* or *near application*.

There is a considerable difference, however, between the content and style of a Year 1 reading book and notices in the street, or the counter signs in a shop, or the advertisements in a window. There are differences of size, colour, vocabulary, typeface and so on. The word 'toy' in the reading book is presented as simply, clearly and consistently as possible. The word 'toy' in shops in the high street comes in a potentially bewildering variety of forms and decorations. The capacity to make sense across widely differing contexts such as these is said to demand the *far transfer* or *far application* of knowledge and skill.

Applying mathematical knowledge

As we have just seen, many learners in many settings seem to have or acquire a ready capacity for near and far transfer or application of knowledge and skill. This seems particularly so in the case of reading. But it is spectacularly not so in the case of mathematics.

Just as for reading, so we learn mathematics in school with a view to going beyond classroom exercises and to using mathematical knowledge and skill in all relevant aspects of our professional and domestic lives. Here, unfortunately, and in sharp contrast to reading, we find learners are not at all fluent in application. People seem to be readily defeated when they meet situations that vary, sometimes by very little, from those they meet in their classroom exercises.

Examples of failure to use basic mathematical competences are legion. In one national mathematics survey, for example, it was found that 80 per cent of 12-year-olds could quickly and correctly divide 225 by 15. However, only 40 per cent of the same sample could solve the problem 'if a gardener had 225 bulbs to place equally in 15 flower beds, how many would be put in each bed?' Most of the failing pupils did not know which mathematical procedure to use, although they were capable of conducting the routine once the appropriate process was named.

Another well known example comes from a survey of mathematical understanding carried out in the USA in the 1980s (National Assessment of Educational Progress 1983). As part of this survey, 13-year-old students were told that an army bus holds 36 soldiers and asked how many buses would be needed to transport 1128 soldiers to their training site. Most of the students knew that they needed to carry out a division calculation, and many successfully divided 1128 by 36 to produce an answer of 31.33. However, nearly a third of the students proceeded to write 31.33 as the answer to the problem, thus ignoring the need for a whole number of buses. Nearly a quarter of the students made a different kind of mistake and ignored the remainder altogether, thus leaving 12 soldiers with no transport.

Sometimes changes merely in the layout of a question are sufficient to throw people. After experience of calculations laid out as in (a) below, many pupils are defeated by the layout shown in (b).

Find x:
(a) $9 + 7 = x$
(b) $9 + x = 16$

Find x:
(a) $\dfrac{24}{8} = x$
(b) $\dfrac{24}{x} = 3$

Clearly, people often show a very limited capacity to use or apply mathematics. It might be felt that the matter could be dismissed by arguing that the people who fail simply have a rather weak grasp of the basic skills in mathematics. But this is not the case. This was evident in a study of some Swedish 12- and 13-year-olds who were accomplished at basic mathematics (Säljö and Wyndhamn 1990). In this study the pupils were asked to find the cost of posting a letter. They were given the letter (which weighed 120 grams), some scales and a simple post office chart showing rates of postage. For example, letters up to 100 grams would cost 4 kronor, while letters up to 250 grams would cost 7.5 kronor. This is in fact a very simple problem, requiring only that the letter be weighed and the appropriate rate read off from the chart. However, many of the pupils failed to find the correct cost of postage and most of those who succeeded did so after a great deal of trouble. The higher the mathematical attainment of the pupils, the more roundabout were their problem-solving procedures. These pupils, it seemed, had considerable difficulty in knowing which aspect of their classroom knowledge to apply to this 'real world' problem. Even these accomplished youngsters showed severe limitations in their capacity to use or apply their mathematical knowledge and skills from one setting to another.

A further illustration of the problem of application comes from a study of Brazilian children's mathematical competencies described by Nunes *et al.* (1993). The children in question were street traders in a large Brazilian city. Street trading is an economic necessity for large numbers of urban youngsters in Brazil. Children trade in fruit, cigarettes, paper goods, drinks and a wide range of other low cost goods. Trading involves purchasing goods from a variety of wholesalers, pricing the goods to sell in a variety of units (for example single items or multiple item packs) and selling the goods, which involves calculating the price of complex purchases and the change due to the customers. An added complication for the children was that Brazil's inflation rate at the time of the study was 250 per cent per annum and, as a consequence, selling not only had to make a straight profit but a profit allowing for the inflated cost of restocking.

Nunes and her colleagues studied several of these children in the working environment of their street stalls. Only one of the children had more than four years of schooling. The children's capabilities were first observed in normal trading transactions, for example:

Customer/researcher:	How much is one coconut?
Trader:	Thirty-five.
Customer:	I'd like ten. How much is that?
Trader:	(Pause) Three will be one hundred and five; with three more, that will be two hundred and ten. (Pause) I need four more. That is . . . (Pause) three hundred and fifteen . . . I think it is three hundred and fifty.

(Nunes *et al.* 1993: 18–19)

In all, 63 problems were set in this way to five traders aged between 9 and 15 years. Overall, the traders had a success rate of 98 per cent. Next, the same children were presented with formal arithmetic tests. For these tests the items were exactly the same as those met on the streets, except that they were reduced to the arithmetic question only. For example, instead of asking, 'What is the cost of ten coconuts at 35 each?', the trader was given pencil and paper and asked 'What is 10 × 35?' With these tests the children had a great deal more difficulty. Their success rate fell from 98 per cent in the mental arithmetic of the street to 37 per cent in the formal 'school test'.

On the surface, the Brazilian children and the Swedish children might seem to have the reverse problem to each other. The Brazilian children have trouble transferring their street knowledge to the school test, while the Swedish children have trouble applying their school knowledge to the 'street' problem. However, we could put the problem another way. We could say that both groups of children have trouble in applying mathematical expertise learned in one setting to problems posed in another context.

Whichever way we look at it, the examples serve powerfully to illustrate a well known problem of mathematics education wherever it is fostered. People seem to have enormous difficulty in using and applying mathematical skills and knowledge from the instructions and formats in which they are learned to novel situations. This poses a major challenge to a key area of schooling, that key aim being to make the lessons of school applicable to the larger world of everyday life.

Applying knowledge in other subjects

It should not be assumed that mathematics is the only area of the school curriculum in which there is evidence of pupils' difficulties in using and applying knowledge and skills. The problem is evident in many other areas of the curriculum.

One of our students reported that in a PE lesson she had taught her class the skills of lifting heavy, cumbersome objects safely: back straight, knees bent, load held securely at its base, and so on. The pupils were good at using these skills in the school hall whenever it was necessary to get out or put away PE apparatus, but they never used the skills spontaneously when moving large pieces of classroom furniture.

Another student reported teaching pupils several approaches to ball passing, including loop passes, bounce passes and feinting. Once the pupils returned to the context of a game of netball, however, the usual maelstrom ensued and it was as if the lesson on passing had never existed. There was a complete failure to transfer to a real game skills that had been clearly demonstrated in skill-focused lessons.

As these examples suggest, the problem of application is widely evident and deep seated. It has a long history of perplexing the teaching profession. Our concern here will be with the mathematics curriculum, and with teaching and learning mathematics. In the remainder of this chapter our focus will be on taking a closer look at the problem of application and at previous attempts to understand it. A solution to the problem must rest on clear understanding.

Understanding knowledge application

To understand knowledge application, it is necessary to understand first the nature of knowledge and its acquisition. When we learn a subject, what is it that we learn and how do we learn it? These questions raise wide-ranging issues in both philosophy and psychology. It is not our intention here to comment exhaustively on these matters. It is necessary, however, to consider some of the perspectives that have been used to understand the problem, and to give particular attention to their implications for teachers and for learners.

Here we will look briefly at three views on the nature of knowledge in mathematics. We have chosen these perspectives because they have had, and continue to have, a major influence on mathematics teaching. There are many other perspectives on the matter, but space does not allow a fuller treatment. The three perspectives are:

- associationism;
- constructivism;
- situated cognition.

In each case we will raise and comment on the following questions:

1 What is the nature of knowledge from this perspective; what is it that has to be learned?
2 What is the difference between an expert and a novice from this perspective?
3 How does the change from novice to expert come about; what is the nature of learning?
4 How is the problem of application conceptualized within this perspective?
5 What implications does this perspective have for teaching?

Associationism

From this perspective, knowledge consists of making connections or associations between small elements of experience. We link words with things or experiences. For example, we hear 'hot' as we burn ourselves and store the link in memory. The next time we hear 'hot' we anticipate the burning experience. We link the word 'two' with the symbol '2', or with the perception of two objects.

All learning, however complex, is in this view made up of associations. In mathematics, for example, the long multiplication of, say, 127×16, can be seen to be made up of a large number of links involving the basic connections of 6×7, 6×2, 6×1, 1×7, 1×2, and 1×1, together with connections of place, value and associations of layout on the page. With this view of knowledge, the difference between an expert and a novice at mathematics is that the expert has a larger and richer corpus of associations between the basic links of mathematics (such as $1 \times 1 = 1$) and the bigger patterns and processes of mathematics (such as 127×16).

From the associationist perspective, learning involves acquiring more links or connections and having them at ready disposal, preferably automatically. Learning proceeds according to the 'laws of association' (Thorndike 1913), which define the conditions under which connections in experience are most readily made and sustained, or remembered, or used appropriately. Links or connections are best made when the elements to be linked are experienced together. This is called the 'law of contiguity'. A simple example is that it helps to link $1 + 1 = 2$ if, whenever $1 + 1$ is met, the symbol '2' is seen or the word 'two' is heard. Repetition also helps to establish links. This is the 'law of practice'. Active use by the learner (practice) is helpful if it is accompanied by positive feedback. For example, for the novice mathematician in a reception class this involves a teacher saying 'good' whenever they complete the link $1 + 1 = 2$, or a teacher saying 'one add one equals two' whenever an error is made or there is too long a delay in making the link. Repeated practice of perfect performance is known to help association to become automatic. Experts in any field practice skills and knowledge-use over and over again to secure 'over-learning'.

The teacher's role, from the associationist point of view, is straightforward. First, the curriculum must be 'unpacked' into its many associations and links until the basic associations are identified. For example, all complex procedures in mathematics can be analysed down to the four basic rules of number. A learning sequence is then designed so that the pupil meets mathematical problems first in their simplest elements. Only when pupils are fluent with the basic associations of mathematics do they move to the next level of associations. For example, pupils first learn number names. Then they learn basic addition bonds – the so-called number bonds – to 10, that is $1 + 1, 1 + 2 \ldots$ until they are familiar with $9 + 1, 8 + 2$, and so on. Subtraction bonds are then learned within this small quantity range. Indeed, they should be over-learned until the presence of the left-hand side of the equation (for example, $3 + 2$) automatically leads to the right-hand side of the equation (5 in this case). When automaticity is achieved in horizontal layout, pupils might advance to vertical layout:

$$
\begin{array}{ll}
1 & 1 \\
+\,1 & +\,2 \\
\hline
2 & 3
\end{array}
$$

It can be seen that little is left to chance. Little transfer or application is anticipated in this perspective. There is a 'law of identical elements' in association theory, which in essence says that you can expect transfer from one problem to another to the degree that they have identical elements in common. So given that a pupil can say '1 dog add 1 dog makes 2 dogs', transfer might be expected to '1 cat add 1 cat makes 2 cats', although success would be by no means certain.

Once teachers have arranged the teaching sequence or, more commonly, bought workbooks arranged in the appropriate sequence, their job is to manage lots of demonstration followed by practice with feedback. Lessons would typically take the form of the teacher showing the association and then getting the pupils to repeat it in various examples, changing only the content used (for example, dogs, cats, pencils, counters, toys, people). The basic association (for example, $7 + 3 = 10$) should stay the same. The teacher then requires the pupils to work on their own, conducting 'massed practice' – that is to say, very long sessions of practice on the same association – giving feedback as appropriate until it is perfectly evolved.

As new associations are added to the repertoire, revision of old associations becomes necessary, using practice with feedback. Again, little transfer is expected. Learning is the accumulation of associations. Successful performance on a 'new' problem depends, from the associationist perspective, on the degree of familiarity of the elements of the problem with associations already held in mind. Practice and structured experience arranged by teachers best equip their pupils for success in mathematics.

Evidence shows that pupils show more transfer than is expected from a strictly associationist perspective. In one study of the performance of algebraic functions, pupils were taught to solve problems such as $(x + y)^2$. In a test of transfer they were given problems such as $(b_1 + b_2)^2$. In the training condition there were 6 per cent errors, while in the transfer condition there were 28 per cent errors (Singley and Anderson 1989). Clearly, pupils experience difficulties here, but they are not so overwhelmed as the 'identical elements' theory would predict.

Constructivism

Constructivist psychologists (such as Piaget) take the view that we learn little of any importance through simple associations. Rather, they suggest that human learners have the capacity to invent or construct general theories about their experience. These theories then enable them to apply structures learned in one situation to a large range of situations of different concrete content but the same intellectual structure (Piaget 1972). For example, pupils might learn that A is bigger than B and B is bigger than C. They then work out, without necessary concrete experience, that A must be bigger than C. Once they have this logical structure it can be predicted that they will be able to transfer it to any problems with three elements, regardless of whether the relationship is 'bigger', 'faster' or 'longer' (Piaget and Inhelder 1966).

Pupils are perceived, from the constructivist perspective, not merely to react to experience but to reflect on it or theorize it and, through logic, to develop mental structures or schemas for understanding it. A large number of such structures have been studied by Piagetian psychologists, of which perhaps the best known is 'conservation of number' (Piaget 1952). This topic has received intense scrutiny from psychologists, and many of Piaget's original claims about conservation have been challenged. Our purpose here is not to enter this debate, but to use conservation of number as an illustration of the child's capacity for construction.

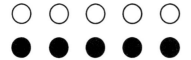

Figure 1.1   Array of counters used to assess children's conservation of number

In a typical conservation task, children are presented with the array of counters shown in Figure 1.1 and asked if there are the same number in each row. Children aged around 4–5 years, like older children, will usually say 'Yes'. If the extreme right black counter is moved an inch or so to the right and the same question is asked, older children (aged say 7–8 years) will say 'Yes' but younger children (aged say 4–5 years) will usually say 'No'. The younger ones, it is argued, judge the number of counters by the length of the array, rather than by using a number operation.

At some later stage children may apply their emerging knowledge of counting to the problem. When children at this stage meet the above test they frequently hesitate, and will sometimes judge the extended row of black counters to have the same number of counters as the row of white counters, and sometimes judge it to be more. It is hypothesized that the children have two ways of answering the question. Firstly they look at the extension of the array and conclude that the black row contains more than the white row. Secondly they count the counters in both arrays and conclude that there is the same number in each array.

At a later stage still, children reliably conclude that both arrays have the same number regardless of their pattern of distribution. When asked for a reason for this judgement they say that in moving the counters, nothing has been added or taken away. This reveals that the children have invented or constructed a way of thinking about the problem that goes beyond looking at the arrays and goes beyond counting the counters. They have invented the concept of the conservation of number. That is to say, they have invented the idea that some processes influence quantity (adding or subtracting items) and some processes do not (changing the distribution). Constructivist psychologists then argue that such intellectual structures can transfer to any problem involving number processing or other quantitative processes.

From a constructivist perspective, learning consists of the invention of increasingly powerful logical structures for dealing with experience. Such structures of thought run across the curriculum and can be applied to science, mathematics, humanities and the arts, as appropriate. The difference between a novice and an expert in this perspective is qualitative rather than quantitative. The expert knows 'different' rather than 'more'. The expert has more powerful ways of structuring experience and these ways have more general application. Once the logic of a situation has been grasped the precise contents are not, from this perspective, so important. Transfer or application should flow across all problems of the same type.

The change from novice to expert is not easily attained. Learning consists of the restructuring of intellectual schemas. The processes involved are shown in Figure 1.2. In understanding the diagram it may be useful to refer back to the account of young children's acquisition of the schema of number conservation.

Initially the child has a schema for number (involving looking at distribution) that causes no problems. The child is said to be in a state of equilibrium. But learning to count and being questioned provide the child with data that do not fit this schema. The experience causes disequilibrium. The child might ignore this or learn to live with the conflict. There is extensive evidence that this is what learners at all ages and stages frequently do in the face of challenges to existing schema. Under these circumstances no learning takes place. Even if the learner takes the conflicting data seriously, he or she still has to invent a new structure to achieve progress. The new structure, like a new scientific theory, has to cope with all the old evidence as well as the new evidence. You will see that the invention of the logic 'if nothing is added or nothing taken away then the number is the same' achieves this for the young learner.

From a constructivist perspective, teaching involves understanding learners' intellectual development; being able to identify existing schemas, and then arranging experiences that challenge those schemas and provide the construction of more advanced intellectual structures. None of these tasks are easy and learners have often proved very resistant to such treatments.

In science, for example, many young children believe that shadows are projected through the eyes from the front of the body, that they exist in the dark (although of course you cannot see them) and that they are rather like mirror images. A constructivist approach to teaching a more established view of shadows is to pose challenges to the young learners' theory. They can be shown and asked to explain how shadows move even though the observer does not. They can be shown double shadows. These techniques are known to create disequilibrium but they do not necessarily lead to new constructions. Once new constructions are created, however,

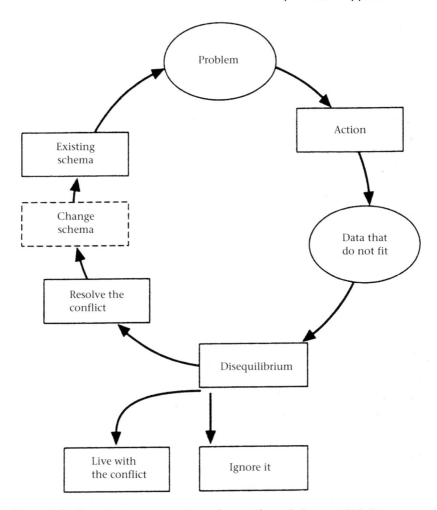

Figure 1.2   Learning as restructuring schemas (from G. Brown 1995: 21)

constructivist psychologists expect them to be very powerful and to be at the heart of knowledge application.

For example, young learners are known to construct a schema for conservation of quantity of substance. This leads them to understand that the amount of substance (such as the quantity of Plasticine in a ball) stays the same whether the ball is squashed or rolled out or re-shaped into a cake. The simple test is, 'Is anything added or taken away in this transformation?' Such a powerful logic is expected to apply to all materials under any and all transformations and to constitute clear exemplification of knowledge application.

Sadly, and somewhat perplexing perhaps, learners who confidently conserve quantity and appear to have invented the basic rule for themselves do not necessarily apply their thinking to other, related problems. They are easily fooled by change of materials. For example, what applies to Plasticine does not necessarily apply to sand or salt. And some transformations, such as cutting the quantity, seem readily to lead to the schema being abandoned. In short, just as learners show a lot more capacity to transfer knowledge than associationists predict, they show a lot less capacity to transfer than constructivists anticipate. We might conclude that there is something both general and specific involved in knowledge application.

Situated cognition

From both the associationist and constructivist perspectives there is an assumption that something called 'knowledge' can be picked up and abstracted from a situation or experience, stored in the mind or body, and used or applied in a new situation given appropriate clues. In the case of associationism the knowledge takes the form of a connection or a link. The connection is stored in the nervous system and something in the new situation evokes the 'old' or stored knowledge. In the case of constructivism a theory is stored in the mind of the learner, and something in the new situation provokes the learner to see the relevance of the extant theory. In both these perspectives, what we know can be separated from the situation in which we first came to know it; the learning situation.

Some psychologists (for example Brown *et al.* 1989) do not accept this view. They argue that knowledge cannot be separated from the context in which we learn it. Learning, in their view, is a fundamentally social activity, which is defined by the culture and context of the learning setting. They say that knowledge is 'situated' in the context of learning.

This perspective helps to explain why the Brazilian children could not transfer their street knowledge to the formal tests. From the perspective of situated cognition, practising mathematics on the street needed all the clues and cues of the street: the objects to hand; customers; vending relationships; and immediacy. The same perspective may also explain why the Swedish children could not transfer their classroom competence to the real-world postage problem. Instead, the children transferred their practices of classroom work, most of which were inappropriate to the new setting, and made it more difficult than it really was.

From the perspective of situated cognition, we do not learn connections as suggested by the associationists, nor do we create theories as suggested by the constructivists. Rather, we learn the working practices of the setting in which we operate. The Brazilian children learned the working practices of the street traders, while the Swedish children learned the working practices of school lessons. Neither group was well equipped to use or apply or transfer the working practices from one setting to another. Indeed, by definition, working practices do not transfer from one culture or activity to another.

Knowledge, then, from the perspective of situated cognition, consists of the working practices of a culture of learning. Science is what scientists do, while mathematics is made up of the working practices of mathematicians. Experts are polished exponents of the working practices of a particular subject group. Experts have become deeply familiar with the ways of working of their profession. Pupils become exponents of classroom work.

Novices must be inducted into the working practices of the domain in question through a form of apprenticeship. Pupils and students will not, from the perspective of situated cognition, learn to use and apply their knowledge met in classrooms if it is met in the form of ordinary classroom work structured by textbooks and work cards. If pupils are to be enabled to apply their knowledge beyond the classroom then they must, from this perspective, learn through authentic experience of the subject in question. As far as possible, it is argued, pupils and students must learn mathematics through being an apprentice mathematician, and meeting problems in the ways mathematicians might experience them.

The teacher's job is to arrange these forms of intellectual apprenticeship as far as is possible. One example of this comes from the work of Schoenfeld, as described by Brown *et al.* (1989). In this example the teacher presented the pupils with the 'magic square' problem (see Figure 1.3), where the pupils are required to place the numbers 1, 2, 3, 4, 5, 6, 7, 8 and 9 in the box so that the sum of each row, column and diagonal is the same.

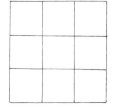

Figure 1.3   The 'magic square' problem (from Schoenfeld, in Brown *et al.* 1989: 38)

The problem is relatively straightforward. However, the collaborative work involved in solving and, more importantly, analysing the problem helped the class to understand how mathematicians look at problems. The class was encouraged to use and discuss a number of approaches, not only to solving the problem, but more basically to understanding the mathematical nature of the challenge. In a typical school task the matter is ended when the specific problem is solved, but in this task the class explored the structure of the problem; they tested their thinking through devising other possible magic squares, and through this they discovered the general principles of the problem. By following through in this way the teacher converts a relatively ordinary school task into a task authentic to the working practices of mathematicians.

An important principle in this approach to teaching is that the class must be actively involved in the work. The teacher does not announce the approaches to be adopted from the front of the class. Rather, the students are encouraged and supported to explore, collectively, systematic ways of understanding and generalizing the problem. In this way the students are exposed to the authentic ways of thinking in the culture of mathematics as much as, if not more so, to its subject matter.

Overview

In this chapter we have introduced the problem of knowledge application, especially as it relates to mathematics. We have also introduced three different theoretical perspectives on the problem: associationism; constructivism; and situated cognition. These three perspectives provide quite different ways of understanding the nature of the problem. They also have very different implications for how application might be addressed in the classroom.

The next chapter will look at how application has been dealt with in the mathematics curriculum in England and Wales. One question we will ask concerns the extent to which approaches taken to application within the curriculum are based on particular theoretical perspectives on learning, such as those described here. In later chapters we will be looking at how application is perceived by some teachers in English primary schools, and at ways in which they develop their practice in this area. Again, we will be asking about the extent to which the approaches taken by the teachers – and the ways in which they themselves 'theorize' the problem – fit with the psychological theories and teaching solutions described in this chapter.

Application in the mathematics curriculum

In this chapter we look at the way in which application has been treated within the mathematics curriculum in England and Wales. We start with the period before 1988, when the National Curriculum was introduced, and look at some of the concerns that led to its introduction. Next, we look at the ways in which application has been treated within the different versions of the National Curriculum. We pay particular attention here to the advice given to teachers about 'Using and Applying Mathematics', and at the ways in which this area of the curriculum has been interpreted by teachers. Finally, we look at the current drive to raise standards in numeracy, and at the place application occupies within the National Numeracy Strategy. Our concern throughout is not just with what is specified in the curriculum, but also with the extent to which the curriculum reflects a particular theoretical approach to the problem of application.

The build-up to the National Curriculum

The mathematics curriculum for state schools in England and Wales is defined by law and embodied in the National Curriculum. The National Curriculum was set up in the context of acute political concern regarding standards of attainment in state education in general and mathematics attainment in particular. However, concern about standards of attainment in mathematics has had a very long history. Indeed, from the very inception of government funding for state education, inspectors' reports have criticized the poor standards achieved in both basic arithmetic and problem solving. There has also been enduring criticism from employers regarding poor levels of numeracy and problem-solving abilities among school leavers.

Brown (1996) has traced the recent history of the mathematics curriculum for state schools. It is, as she shows, a history of increasing political involvement. Prior to the 1970s, the curricula for secondary schools were largely determined by the syllabuses of public examination boards, while the curricula for primary schools were mainly determined by individual teachers' preferences. During the 1970s, however, various attempts were made to centralize the content of the mathematics curriculum. In 1977, for example, Her Majesty's Inspectors (HMI) recommended a curriculum for the 11–16 age range that contained eight 'areas of experience', one of which was mathematics (DES 1977). The emphasis, to a large degree, was on the promotion of understanding, communication and reasoning in mathematics, rather than on routine calculating. This emphasis on processes was more clearly evident in the subsequent HMI advisory document for the primary age range, where a broad, practical curriculum was suggested (DES 1979). These discussion documents, however, had no statutory force, and individual schools made what they wished of them.

At the end of the 1970s, the government set up a Committee of Inquiry into the teaching of mathematics in schools. This action was prompted, among other things, by persistent criticism from employers about the mathematical attainment of school leavers. The findings of the inquiry were published in 1982, and became widely known as the Cockcroft Report, after the chair of the committee (Cockcroft 1982). Significantly, the Cockcroft Report found an almost universal lack of confidence in mathematics among the adult population, and an equal lack of ability in applying mathematical knowledge or using it to communicate effectively. To address these problems the report recommended that the mathematics curriculum in schools and the assessment procedures of examination boards should be broadened to include more practical work, problem solving and investigations. The focus was to be on enhancing the applicability of the school curriculum.

Brown (1996) suggests that the Cockcroft Report had considerable impact not only on examination board syllabuses but also on examination processes and procedures. There was strong support for coursework components in assessment, and schools began to develop and enhance project work and investigations. Such developments, it seems, did not diminish the political interest in determining the curriculum of state schools. Concern about standards remained and was explicit in the 1985 White Paper *Better Schools*, where it was claimed that 'the standards now generally attained by our pupils are neither as good as they can be, nor as good as they need to be' (DES 1985: sec. 9). It was also maintained that comparative studies of mathematics attainment across nations revealed relatively poor performances by English and Welsh pupils. Assumptions were readily made about the relationship between economic performance, educational attainment and curriculum reform. The stage was set for the introduction of a statutory National Curriculum.

Application in the National Curriculum

The first version of the National Curriculum in mathematics contained long lists of content to be covered (DES 1989a). The programme of study was organized into 14 attainment targets, two of which referred explicitly to 'using and applying mathematics'. Attainment Target 1 (AT1) stated that *'pupils should use number, algebra and measures in practical tasks, in real-life problems, and to investigate within mathematics itself'* (p. 3). In a similar fashion, Attainment Target 9 (AT9) stated that *'pupils should use shape and space and handle data in practical tasks, in real-life problems and to investigate within mathematics itself'* (p. 23).

The more detailed statements of attainment made it clear that these two attainment targets were essentially concerned with the *processes* of mathematics. For example, it was expected that pupils at Level 2 – the modal level in Key Stage 1 – would be able to:

- select the materials and the mathematics to use for a task;
- describe current work, record findings and check results;
- ask and respond to the question: 'What would happen if . . . ?'

(DES 1989a: 3)

Similarly, it was expected that pupils at Level 4 – the modal level in Key Stage 2 – would be able to:

- select the materials and the mathematics to use for a task; plan work methodically;
- record findings and present them in oral, written or visual form, as appropriate;
- use examples to test statements or definitions.

(DES 1989a: 4)

The 1989 version of the National Curriculum was considered by many to have lowered the status of application through the heavy weighting on content. In particular, it was seen as a move away from the Cockcroft emphasis on processes and practical mathematics. However, this perception was not supported by the 'non-statutory guidance', which was issued by the National Curriculum Council (NCC) to accompany the curriculum into schools. This guidance clearly stated that:

> The National Curriculum requires all schools . . . to develop a teaching and learning approach in which the uses and application of mathematics permeate and influence all work in mathematics. This

is a major undertaking for schools, and perhaps the single most significant challenge for the teaching of mathematics required by the National Curriculum in its aim of raising standards for schools.

(DES 1989b: D5)

The 1989 version of the National Curriculum in mathematics posed considerable problems for those charged with developing materials and procedures for its assessment. It quickly became apparent that the idea of assessing all 14 attainment targets was impractical. It was therefore decided that the curriculum for mathematics (and for science, which was experiencing similar problems) should be revised during 1991. This revision concentrated on changes to the structure rather than the content of the curriculum. As a result, the 1991 version of the National Curriculum (DES 1991) consisted of only five attainment targets. Attainment Targets 1 and 9 were amalgamated into a single attainment target entitled 'Using and Applying Mathematics' (AT1). Within this attainment target, the three strands of *applications, mathematical communication* and *reasoning, logic and proof* were explicitly identified for the first time. However, the detailed statements of attainment remained largely unchanged.

From 1991 to 1993 there was growing unrest among the teaching population in England and Wales. Dissatisfaction was increasingly expressed about the heavily specified content of the National Curriculum and about the arrangements for the standardized assessment of pupils. In 1993 Sir Ron Dearing was asked to carry out a wholesale revision of the National Curriculum, and to make substantial reductions to its content. As a result of the Dearing Review, a third version of the National Curriculum for mathematics appeared in 1995.

In the 1995 version of the mathematics curriculum, pupils in Key Stage 1 were expected to make progress on three attainment targets: 'Using and Applying Mathematics'; 'Number'; and 'Shape, Space and Measures' (DfE 1995). For Key Stage 2 pupils, a further attainment target, 'Handling Data', was added. At the same time, the official documents made it clear that the attainment targets were set in a programme of study that should be seen as an integrated whole. In particular, 'Using and Applying Mathematics' was intended to refer to all aspects of pupils' experience.

The 1995 version of 'Using and Applying Mathematics' showed relatively few changes from those of 1989 and 1991. For example, it was explicitly stated that at all key stages *'pupils should be given opportunities to use and apply mathematics in practical tasks, in real-life problems and within mathematics itself'* (DfE 1995: 2). More detailed requirements were laid out under the three strands of: making and monitoring decisions to solve problems; developing mathematical language and communication; and developing mathematical reasoning. Further detail was provided in the level descriptions, which spelt out what was expected of pupils at each of eight levels. Thus, at Level 2 it was expected that:

Pupils select the mathematics for some classroom activities. They discuss their work using familiar mathematical language and are beginning to represent it using symbols and simple diagrams. They ask and respond appropriately to questions including 'What would happen if . . . ?'

(p. 23)

The description for Level 4 was:

Pupils are developing their own strategies for solving problems and are using these strategies both in working within mathematics and in applying mathematics to practical contexts. They present information and results in a clear and organised way, explaining the reasons for their presentation. They search for a pattern by trying out ideas of their own.

(p. 23)

It is clear that, despite the various revisions to the National Curriculum, there are some consistent ideas about how application in mathematics might be fostered. All versions of the National Curriculum state that pupils should be given opportunities to use and apply mathematics in practical tasks, in real-life problems and within mathematics itself. All versions give central importance to the three processes of decision making, communication and reasoning. All versions provide detailed statements of what is meant by these processes at different stages of the curriculum. At the same time, the rationale for this particular approach to application is never clearly spelt out. Rather, the designers of the National Curriculum appear to assume that, if children are taught along the lines suggested, then they will have few problems in applying their mathematical knowledge.

Teaching 'Using and Applying Mathematics'

It quickly became clear that the ideas contained in the National Curriculum concerning using and applying mathematics were causing problems for teachers. An HMI report on the first year of implementation reported that:

Many schools had difficulty with . . . [AT1, which is] concerned with the processes of using and applying mathematics, because there had been little emphasis on these areas in the past. It was generally considered easier to fill 'content gaps' than to develop a mathematics curriculum in which . . . [this attainment target] underpinned all the mathematical work done by the pupils.

(HMI 1991)

The organization then in charge of implementing the curriculum, the National Curriculum Council (NCC), acted quickly in response to this and other evidence. Materials were produced to help teachers understand the meaning of AT1, and to help them integrate AT1 into the broader mathematics curriculum. These materials described in detail what was meant by the three main strands of applications, mathematical communication and reasoning, logic and proof, and explained how teachers might plan activities to cover them (NCC 1992). Ironically enough, these NCC materials were not widely distributed, due to a moratorium on circulating curriculum documents to schools. Nevertheless, the advice contained in the materials is worth looking at more closely, as it provides some very detailed guidance on how application might be taught.

The *application* strand of AT1 required pupils to make decisions about the sort of problem they were dealing with and the techniques, methods and apparatus that might be brought to bear on it. Having made choices in these respects, pupils were expected to monitor their progress on the problem, to evaluate how close they were to a solution and, where appropriate, to change their approach. These ideas are far-reaching and involve considerations that go beyond mathematics. For example, pupils need to be able to stand back from a problem, to have the confidence to refine it or restate it, to decide what sort of records to keep to aid progress and to choose a working style, such as whether to work independently or in a group.

In promoting the development and use of these capabilities, the NCC materials made it clear that teachers must design tasks that require appropriate pupil engagement. Tasks must be carefully designed both to require and, to some degree, constrain pupils' choices and strategies. For example, pupils might be required to 'make a box'. This potentially offers a bewildering range of possibilities in terms of scale, size, purpose, materials and range of mathematical knowledge of shape, space and measure. The basic task is very open-ended and could usefully be set for able mathematicians. On the other hand it can also be constrained for younger pupils or those with less experience. In one example, Year 8 pupils were asked to design a matchbox, which had to 'hold 45 matches, be made from a single net, and make economical use of materials' (NCC 1992: 14).

The *communication* strand of AT1 required pupils to engage in discussing and reporting on appropriate aspects of a problem. They might consider how the problem is formulated and refined, how progress is to be monitored and how the solutions or findings might best be presented. This might involve describing ideas, understanding each other's points of view and clarifying thoughts. Communication can take many forms of representation, including oral, written, graphical and numerical.

Again, if pupils are to get the most out of their mathematics applications work, teachers must design tasks that require pupils to develop a range of modes of communication, to select a choice of mode as appropriate and to evaluate the effectiveness of various modes through comparison of each other's work. The NCC materials gave the example of a Year 7 pupil called Ian who was set the problem 'Is three times round your head equal to your height?' Ian chose to communicate his findings in the two ways shown below. This opened up the possibility of discussing the advantages and dis-advantages of each representation.

Is three times round your head equal to your height?
Working on this, Ian (Year 7) translated his table of findings into graphical form.

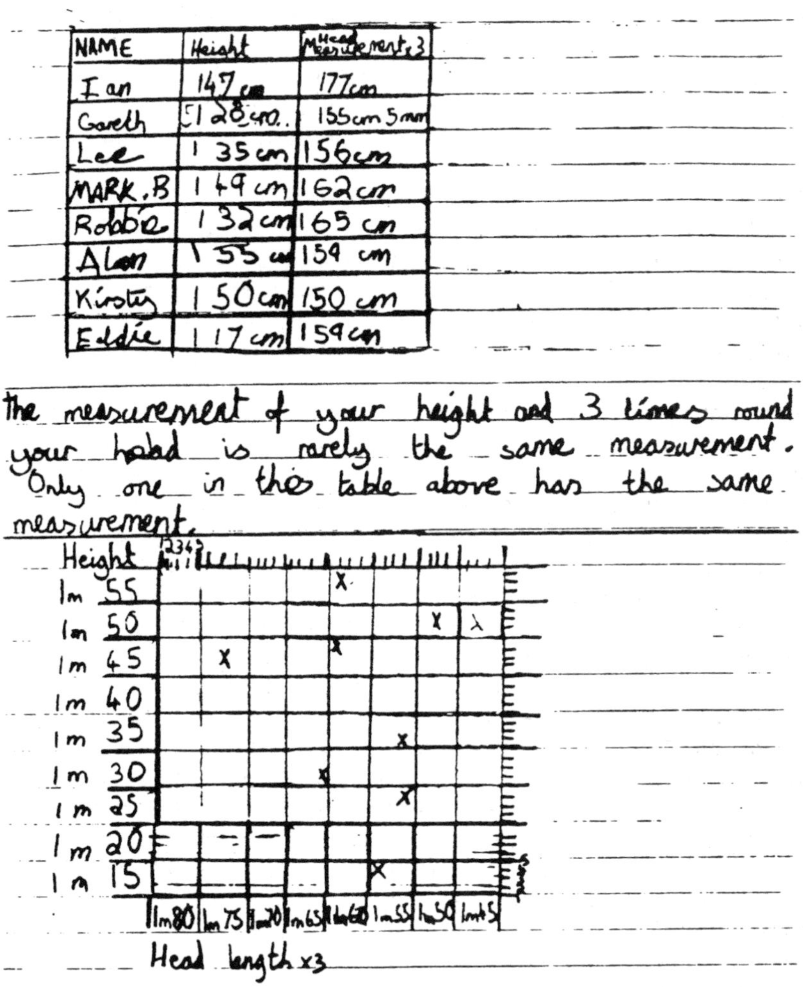

NAME	Height	Head Measurement 3
Ian	147 cm	177 cm
Gareth	128 cm	155 cm 5 mm
Lee	135 cm	156 cm
Mark.B	149 cm	162 cm
Robbie	132 cm	165 cm
Alan	155 cm	159 cm
Kirsty	150 cm	150 cm
Eddie	117 cm	159 cm

The measurement of your height and 3 times round your head is rarely the same measurement. Only one in the table above has the same measurement.

Figure 2.1   Is three times round your head equal to your height? (NCC 1992: 23)

The *reasoning* strand of AT1 concerned pupils' capacity to see relationships, make reasoned arguments and give justifications. It involved the capacities to make and test predictions, to conjecture, to make generalizations and to develop logical proofs. Once again, the teachers' challenge is to design tasks that allow pupils to learn these skills and capabilities and that require pupils to use them.

The NCC materials provided a range of examples of how teachers might do this. For example, illustrations were given of ways in which conjectures or conclusions might proceed from specific cases. In one case, the problem of determining 'how most people arrived at school' was set to a class of Year 3 children. The class proceeded by finding out how each child travelled to school. They then plotted a graph and concluded that most children walked to school. In another instance a Year 9 pupil was asked to find the number of solutions to the problem $\square - \triangle = 10$. The pupil began by generating specific examples such as $20 - 10$, and $15 - 5$. After making up a range of specific cases he came to the general conclusion that 'You can go on and on there is no end' (NCC 1992: 30).

The NCC materials also suggested that a powerful form of mathematical reasoning involved the reverse process using specific cases to test a general conjecture. This was illustrated by the same Year 9 pupil, who had been given the problem of $\triangle \times \triangle = 10$. His first conclusion was 'it is impossible' (*ibid.* 31). He then began to test his conclusion by trying out various solutions on his calculator, using a process of successive approximations until he reached a satisfactory outcome.

Teachers' interpretations of 'Using and Applying Mathematics'

As we have seen, the National Curriculum was installed as a political response to enduring and widespread concerns about low standards of attainment, particularly in mathematics. Successive versions of the National Curriculum placed considerable emphasis on 'using and applying' being at the centre of the mathematics curriculum. Those involved in developing the curriculum were aware that this might require changes in teachers' practice at both primary and secondary level. Detailed guidance, such as the NCC materials, was made available to help teachers make the necessary changes. However, developing a curriculum and providing guidance may not be sufficient to change practice. We therefore need to look at how teachers have interpreted 'using and applying' within the mathematics curriculum, and whether this has led to changes in their approach. It should be noted that there is very little empirical evidence on this matter. In what follows, we draw entirely on the work of Askew and his colleagues (Askew *et al.* 1993; Askew 1996; Johnson and Millett 1996).

As part of a major evaluation of the implementation of the National Curriculum, Askew *et al.* collected questionnaire data from 744 teachers of pupils from Reception to Year 9. They followed up these questionnaires with the intensive interviewing of 32 teachers. These methods produced considerable evidence concerning teachers' thinking, planning and practice.

Askew and his colleagues found there was wide variation in the way teachers interpreted the idea of 'Using and Applying Mathematics'. However, two concepts – *practical* and *relevant* – were particularly associated with this attainment target. At first sight these look to be in line with the statutory requirements, but closer examination reveals some divergence from official intentions and meanings.

In the teachers' minds *relevant* meant 'immediately useful'. Examples provided by the teachers of recent applications work referred mainly to money and measurement. The use of everyday experience (such as shopping, getting out pencils or sharing sweets) was seen as 'relevant', and this was expected to add to pupils' interest and motivation because of the 'real-world' connections. There was little evidence that teachers thought pupils might find relevance in activities that did not have some immediate practical application. As Askew concluded, 'there is a potential conflict between the interpretation of using and applying as "relevant" in this sense of everyday applicability and relevant in the sense of intellectually engaging' (1996: 105).

By *practical* the teachers in the sample mainly indicated some sort of material embodiment involving physical materials or some real-world context. For example, work was 'practical' if it involved using pebbles for sorting, using a queue of children to discuss ordinality or illustrating fractions with real or drawn cakes. In this sense many teachers claimed that a great percentage of their mathematics work was practical.

In the teachers' examples of practical work there was no sense that the tasks had any purpose beyond the practical exercise as such. In one example, a Year 2 teacher had asked the class to measure various parts of their bodies. The pupils were encouraged to try out various means of measurement, but there was no indication that the pupils' methods were compared or discussed. The exercise was seen as 'using and applying' because it was practical, and it was seen as practical because material objects were used in the everyday world. As Askew concluded, 'overall the impression was one of physical activity assumed to lead to mathematical thinking without overtly exploring such thinking' (1996: 106).

In the National Curriculum, 'Using and Applying Mathematics' has been concerned with the process skills of decision making, communication and reasoning. However, Askew *et al.* found little evidence that the teachers were interpreting the attainment target in this way. Only one teacher (of Year 6) talked about the processes of reasoning, logic and proof, and this was the only teacher to offer an example of classroom practice with this focus in mind. Similarly, Askew found little evidence of specific planning to teach 'using and applying': 'the general impression was that either . . . [AT1] was inseparable from all teaching of mathematics or was dealt with in an opportunistic manner. In either case, specific planning was not necessary' (Askew 1996: 109).

This research by Askew and his colleagues indicated a wide gulf between teachers' conceptions of 'using and applying' and those underpinning the National Curriculum. The teachers' interpretations were narrow, focusing on what was 'practical' or 'relevant'. They appeared to neglect both the process skills embedded in AT1 and the need to plan their teaching of these skills. In contrast, as we saw earlier, the NCC guidance identified a range of problem solving, communication and mathematical reasoning skills and indicated the large and complex planning requirements that are necessary if pupils are to acquire these skills. Askew's research suggested that – at least in the early stages of the National Curriculum – these skills were receiving little attention from teachers.

The National Numeracy Strategy

In the second half of the 1990s, concern about standards in mathematics surfaced again. This time the concern was fuelled by a series of inter-national comparisons, which suggested that pupils in England and Wales were performing poorly compared to those from other countries. In 1996 the Office for Standards in Education (Ofsted) published a report, *Worlds Apart?*, which summarized findings from a large number of international comparisons (Reynolds and Farrell 1996). The report concluded that 'per-formance in mathematics in England is relatively poor overall' (p. 52). This was particularly so in relation to countries from the Pacific Rim, such as Korea, Taiwan and Japan.

In 1997 the results of the Third International Mathematics and Science Study (TIMSS) were published. Written tests in mathematics and science were used to compare the performance of 9-year-old pupils in 26 different countries. Again, the main conclusion was that 'pupils in England achieved . . . relatively low scores in mathematics' (Harris *et al.* 1997: ii). As Figure 2.2 shows, pupils in England scored below the international average in four out of six test areas where the focus was on number, measurement and pattern. However, they did perform above the inter-national average in the areas of geometry and data representation.

In the same year as the TIMSS results were published, the incoming Labour government set up new national targets in numeracy and literacy. In numeracy, the target was that by the year 2002, 75 per cent of 11-year-olds would reach the standards expected for their age (Level 4 in the National Curriculum). A Numeracy Task Force was set up to develop a national strategy to reach the government's target. The task force's pre-liminary report, published in January 1998, cited evidence from inter-national comparisons to highlight the poor performance of English

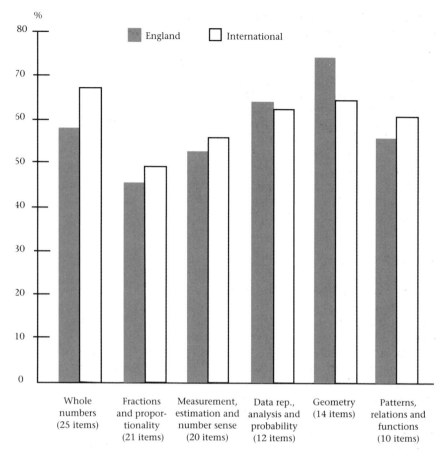

Figure 2.2   Comparison of English Year 5 pupils with the international mean in the TIMSS study (from Harris *et al.* 1997)

primary school children in key aspects of number (DfEE 1998a). At the same time, the report acknowledged that:

> Other data from TIMSS suggest, however, that we also have areas of strength related to numeracy. For example, English pupils are comparatively very successful at applying mathematical procedures to solve practical problems, and have a positive attitude to mathematics as a subject. These are important aspects to preserve while we attempt to raise standards.

> (DfEE 1998a: 8–9)

This first report of the Numeracy Task Force made various proposals for raising standards in numeracy. Its central recommendation was that there should be a daily mathematics lesson in all primary schools lasting for between 45 and 60 minutes. Particular attention within the lesson would be given to oral and mental work in order to develop pupils' calculation strategies and recall skills. More time should also be given to direct communication with pupils, particularly through the use of whole class teaching. In addition, the task force recommended that the National Curriculum for mathematics be modified to place a greater emphasis on oral and mental work 'to secure the foundation of numeracy before formal written methods are introduced' (p. 3). After a period of consultation, these recommendations provided the basis for the task force's final report in July 1998, and they were accepted by the government as the basis of the National Numeracy Strategy.

More detailed guidance on the form as well as the content of the daily mathematics lesson was outlined in a further document, *The National Numeracy Strategy: Framework for Teaching Mathematics from Reception to Year 6* (DfEE 1999, hereafter referred to as the Numeracy Framework). The Numeracy Framework was developed and used in the course of the National Numeracy Project, one of several projects that at that time were developing methods for raising standards of attainment in mathematics. The Framework provides advice for teachers on how a typical lesson should be structured, on the kinds of teaching skills involved in whole class teaching, and on matters of classroom organization. It also provides detailed objectives for each year group in the primary age range, together with a large number of examples of what children in each year should know and be able to do. All in all, the Numeracy Framework provides the most detailed and prescriptive recommendations for teaching primary mathematics ever produced in England and Wales.

As with the National Curriculum, the theoretical basis for the National Numeracy Strategy is by no means clear. For example, there are no explicit references to any particular theory of learning within the reports of the Numeracy Task Force or the Numeracy Framework. The Numeracy Task Force certainly claims that its recommendations are based on research evidence, but the exact nature of this evidence is not made clear. Indeed, there are reasons for thinking that the evidence for some of its recommendations is quite slim (Brown *et al.* 1998). These authors reviewed the research literature in each key area of the National Numeracy Strategy and came to the following conclusion:

> The discussion of whether the recommendations in the National Numeracy Strategy are based on research has shown varied results: sometimes recommendations are quite strongly underpinned, sometimes the evidence is ambiguous, sometimes there is little relevant literature, and sometimes the research is at odds with the recommendations.
>
> (Brown *et al.* 1998: 378)

Application within the National Numeracy Strategy

How is the problem of application perceived and dealt with under the National Numeracy Strategy? How far do the objectives of the Numeracy Framework relate to the notion of 'using and applying mathematics' found in successive versions of the National Curriculum? To answer these questions, we need to look more closely at the key documents underlying the strategy.

The final report of the Numeracy Task Force recommended that the following definition of numeracy be used to underpin the National Numeracy Strategy:

> Numeracy at Key Stages 1 and 2 is a proficiency that involves a confidence and competence with numbers and measures. It requires an understanding of the number system, a repertoire of computational skills and an inclination and ability to solve number problems in a variety of contexts. Numeracy also demands practical understanding of the ways in which information is gathered by counting and measuring, and is presented in graphs, diagrams, charts and tables. This proficiency is promoted through giving a sharper focus to the relevant aspects of the National Curriculum programmes of study for mathematics.
>
> (DfEE 1998b: 11)

This definition suggests that, while numeracy is primarily about skills and knowledge, it is also about the application of these skills and knowledge. This suggestion is further supported by the list of ten numeracy competencies that immediately followed the above definition. Although most of the skills in this list were primarily concerned with number knowledge and calculation, it was nevertheless proposed that numerate primary pupils should be able to:

- make sense of number problems, including non-routine problems, and recognise the operations needed to solve them;
- explain their methods and reasoning using correct mathematical terms;
- explain and make predictions from the numbers in graphs, diagrams, charts and tables.

> (DfEE 1998b: 12)

These skills can be seen to echo key aspects of the three 'using and applying' strands of decision making, communication and reasoning, which feature in all versions of the National Curriculum. However, the exact relationship between the task force's definition of numeracy and mathematics as embodied in the National Curriculum is by no means straightforward. This relationship is addressed by the task force in the following way:

Numeracy is . . . a proficiency in various skills. The National Curriculum for mathematics at each level is in part focused directly upon such skills and in part upon laying the foundation for higher levels of mathematical study which, in turn, provide further skills valuable in adult life.

(p. 11)

This statement suggests that there is more to mathematics than numeracy, and more to the National Curriculum than simply acquiring proficiency in numeracy.

The Numeracy Framework starts from the same definition of numeracy as the Numeracy Task Force. It also lists the same set of ten skills that a numerate primary pupil should be expected to demonstrate. However, the detailed objectives of the Numeracy Framework are presented within a structure of five main strands: numbers and the number system; calculations; solving problems; measures, shape and space; and handling data. These five strands are shown diagrammatically in Figure 2.3.

As Figure 2.3 makes clear, there is no longer a separate programme of study within the Numeracy Framework for 'using and applying mathematics'. However, it is claimed that:

Using and applying mathematics is integrated throughout [original emphasis]: for example, in making and justifying decisions about which method, equipment or unit of measurement to use; in describing properties of numbers or shapes and reasoning about them; in explaining methods of calculation; in devising and refining methods of recording calculations; in checking results . . .

(DfEE 1999: 40)

It is indeed possible to trace links between some of the elements of the National Curriculum programme of study and the content of the Numeracy Framework. For example, it is possible to map the main 'using and applying' elements on to the 'solving problems' strand of the Numeracy Framework, as shown in Figure 2.4.

The stated intention of the Numeracy Framework is therefore to retain the emphasis on the process skills of 'using and applying' found in the National Curriculum. However, a rather different picture emerges when it is looked at in more detail. For example, the 'key objectives' provided for each year group are almost entirely concerned with calculation and number knowledge, with application getting very little attention indeed. At Year 2, for example, only one of the 13 key objectives relates to the application of numeracy, while at Year 4 the proportion is one in 11. The impression created by these key objectives is that application has little priority within the Numeracy Framework.

A similar picture emerges when we look at the supplement of examples provided within the Numeracy Framework to illustrate what should be

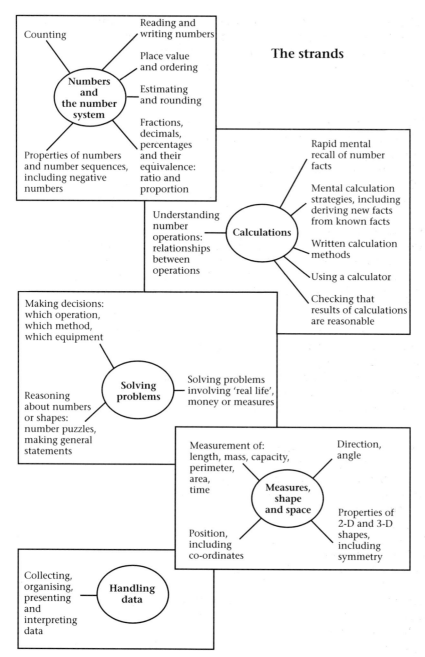

Figure 2.3 The five strands of the Framework (DfEE 1999: 40. Crown copyright reproduced with the permission of the Controller of Her Majesty's Stationery Office)

The Framework third strand 'solving problems'	The National Curriculum Attainment Target 1, 'Using and Applying Mathematics'
Solve problems involving 'real life', money or measures	Use and apply mathematics in practical tasks and 'real life' problems
Make decisions: • which operation • which method • which equipment	Make and monitor decisions to solve problems Select and use the appropriate mathematics and materials
Reason about numbers or shapes: number puzzles, make general statements	Develop mathematical reasoning Make general statements of their own based on evidence they have produced

Figure 2.4   'Using and applying mathematics' and the Numeracy Framework

expected of pupils in each school year. Here we find that, even within the 'solving problems' strand, the emphasis is very much on the practice and use of calculation skills. For example, at Years 4, 5 and 6 a stated objective is that 'pupils should be taught to use all four operations to solve word problems involving numbers in "real life"' (DfEE 1999, section 6: 82). In the Numeracy Framework this is exemplified by a range of problems like the following:

> A beetle has 6 legs.
> How many legs have 9 beetles?
> How many legs have 15 beetles?
>
> (DfEE 1999, section 6: 82)

and

> 960 marbles are put into 16 bags.
> There is the same number of marbles in each bag.
> How many marbles are there in 3 of these bags?
>
> (p. 83)

The connection with 'real life' feels somewhat tenuous in these examples: one might ask, 'Whose real life?' Moreover, it is hard to find in examples like these much trace of the process skills underpinning the 'using and applying' attainment target in successive versions of the National Curriculum. Indeed, there is a marked contrast between these examples and the kind of open-ended problems advocated by the NCC materials described above (pp. 24–6). The examples provided in the Numeracy Framework seem to show a clear movement away from challenging applications work and towards the reinforcement and practice of calculation skills.

Overview

In this chapter we have looked at the way in which application has been treated within the mathematics curriculum of England and Wales. We saw how successive versions of the National Curriculum attempted to address the problem through a separate attainment target and programme of study called 'Using and Applying Mathematics'. We also saw that, despite detailed advice from the NCC and others, 'Using and Applying Mathematics' has been interpreted by teachers in ways that do not necessarily fit with those intended by the architects of the National Curriculum. More recently, the advent of the National Numeracy Strategy has led to a different approach to primary mathematics. Within the Numeracy Framework, 'using and applying mathematics' is no longer a separate strand, although many of the main elements of AT1 can still be identified within the 'solving problems' strand. However, a closer examination of the key objectives of the Numeracy Framework – and the examples given to support these objectives – raises concerns that in practice there will be an overriding emphasis on number knowledge and calculation skills, with relatively little attention being given to application.

How do these approaches to application within the curriculum relate to the three theoretical perspectives described in Chapter 1? It is a notable feature of the many curriculum documents reviewed in this chapter that they contain virtually no explicit references to any theory of learning on which their proposals are based. Nevertheless, it is possible to suggest some connections between theory and curriculum design. For example, the emphasis within the 'using and applying' attainment target on processes such as decision making, communication, reasoning and proof shows some clear resonances with the suggestions from situated cognition that pupils should be apprenticed into the ways in which mathematicians approach problems. In contrast, the approach adopted by the Numeracy Framework, in which the curriculum is broken down into a number of small steps to be presented to pupils in a particular order, together with the emphasis on the repetition and practice of number skills, suggests an approach based on the associationist principles of Thorndike and others. Whether those charged with designing the curriculum would agree with these suggestions is, of course, another matter.

Whatever theoretical ideas about learning are contained within a curriculum, the extent to which they are implemented in the classroom depends crucially on how they are understood and put into practice by teachers themselves. We therefore turn to look at the ways in which primary school teachers conceptualize the problem of application in mathematics, and how they attempt to teach for application in their classrooms.

Teachers' ideas about application

In this chapter and the following ones we will be looking closely at a group of primary school teachers and their approaches to the problem of application. These teachers worked with us during the mid-1990s as part of a research project, 'Using and Applying Mathematical Knowledge in the Primary School', which was funded by the Nuffield Foundation. The main aims of the project were to help the teachers develop their thinking about application and try out different approaches in the classroom. The project centred on a group of 12 teachers from primary schools in the south-west of England. Six of these teachers worked with children at Key Stage 1 (ages 5–7), while six worked with children at Key Stage 2 (ages 7–11). All 12 teachers were considered to be excellent practitioners and were fully committed to developing their practice in mathematics.

Case studies of successful and unsuccessful application

As a starting point for the project, we wanted to elicit the teachers' initial ideas about application. In order to do this, each teacher was asked to provide two written case studies of children working on mathematics in the classroom. One case study was to be of children *successfully* applying their mathematical knowledge, while the other was to be of children who were *unsuccessful* in their application. The teachers were given the following framework as guidance:

- What's the context? What did you give the children?
- What knowledge did you expect them to apply? What evidence do you have that they had this knowledge?

- What actually happened? What did the children do and say? What did you do and say?

The teachers responded to this request in different ways. Some presented a case study of a single activity, which their children had responded to with differing degrees of success. Heather, for example, had given a catalogue shopping list to a group of Year 5 children and asked them to find the approximate total cost of the presents. Some children found this task relatively easy while others found it almost impossible. Other teachers presented case studies of two contrasting activities; one that had 'worked' and one that had not. For example, Diane had asked her Year 1 class to design and make hats for their Christmas party. The activity was successful as the children chose appropriate methods for measuring their heads and for designing the hats on paper. In contrast, when she asked them 'How many more children are having packed lunches than school lunches?', most of the children were unable to apply their knowledge of counting-on or subtraction to the problem.

All the activities chosen by the teachers clearly met the 'using and applying' requirement that 'pupils should be given opportunities to use and apply mathematics in practical tasks, in real-life problems and within mathematics itself' (DfE 1995: 2). Most of the activities fell into the first two of these categories, with the children being asked to apply their knowledge of number to practical problems or 'real-life' situations such as those described above. However, a few of the activities were more open-ended investigations, giving children the opportunity to apply mathematics 'within mathematics itself'. For example, Elaine placed a set of large numbered carpet tiles on the floor, and asked a group of Year 1 children to see how many ways they could 'make 7' with two children each standing on a different tile (2 and 5, 3 and 4, and so on). In another example, Janice used a more complex investigation involving squares. She gave a group of Year 5 children a square made up of nine smaller squares, and asked them to find out how many small squares touched on one edge, two edges, three edges and four edges. She asked them to do this again with squares made of 16 and 25 small squares, and then asked them to make predictions for squares made of 36 and 49 small squares. Essentially she was asking the children to recognize the patterns in their data and use these to make generalizations.

The emphasis given by the project teachers to practical activity of one kind or another reflected the earlier findings of Askew *et al.* (1993), namely that teachers interpret 'using and applying' primarily in terms of activities that are 'practical' or 'relevant' (see Chapter 2, pp. 26–8). At the same time, the project teachers were able to articulate clearly the mathematical knowledge and skills that they expected the children to apply in the case study activities. Moreover, several of their examples suggested that – unlike most of Askew's teachers – they were paying some attention to the processes underlying 'using and applying mathematics', such as decision making, communication and reasoning.

In the remainder of this chapter we consider in detail the case studies provided by two of the project teachers; Claire and Kathy. Claire worked with children at Key Stage 1, while Kathy worked with children at Key Stage 2. These case studies have been chosen because they enable us to raise some central issues concerning teachers' thinking and practice in this area. We do this by asking the following questions:

- What is the nature of the activity?
- How is it intended to promote application?
- What is the teacher's theory of application?
- What does the teacher actually do to promote application?
- What opportunities does the activity present for developing the process skills of decision making, communicating about mathematics and reasoning?

First, we present Claire and Kathy's case studies of successful and unsuccessful application. We then use this set of questions as a basis for comparing and contrasting their approaches to application.

Claire's case of successful application: the wine gums investigation

For her first case study, Claire described an activity that she set for her Year 1 class of 5- and 6-year-olds. At different points throughout the week, groups of four children were given the task of 'finding out' about a packet of wine gums. The class had worked on a similar investigation with Smarties some five weeks previously, with Claire modelling and providing direction on the kinds of things that could be explored with the sweets: sorting, counting, combining groups of different colours, and sharing the Smarties between children. Claire provided the following account of her approach to investigating the box of Smarties:

> [I said to them] 'What shall we do about it? Shall we have a guess and see how many are in the box?' The children agreed and they guessed how many there were in there and then we emptied them into a box and counted them. Then we put them in rows of same colours and we talked about which was most, which colours were most. We matched them with each other and found which had more and how many more and lots and lots of different things, some of which they recorded and some they didn't.

For the investigation with wine gums, Claire wanted the children to apply their knowledge of number, to record graphically and to work on division by sharing. She knew that the children were able to count to 20 and thought they might use this skill during their exploration, possibly finding out how many wine gums there were of each colour. She expected them to share the gums fairly between themselves: 'The sharing, I suppose, was the one thing that I wanted them to do successfully because there would have been uproar if they hadn't!' The task thus provided the children with opportunities to apply their number skills of estimating, counting and sharing within a practical context. They were also required to use the process skills of making decisions about what they were going to do and how they would record their work.

Claire described an episode with one of the groups of children. She presented the task with an open invitation to explore the packet. 'I simply gave them the packet of wine gums and a couple of boxes and said, "There you are, what will you do? You decide what you're going to do and how to record it." I just sat and watched and I didn't answer if they asked me. I just said, "You decide." ' The children began by guessing how many there were before opening the pack. One child recorded their guesses as follows:

14 Amun Natalie Tracy
9 Tony

Natalie counted the wine gums and recorded the actual total of 17. The children then worked on how to share the wine gums between them. Claire observed:

> They decided there was enough for two each and they passed the box round and each took two. Then they said there was enough for one more each. With five left, three children were unsure if there was enough for one more each but Tony persuaded them by saying 'There's five and four of us'.

Reflecting on why the children were successful on this occasion, Claire commented, 'They had done a similar problem before . . . the risk they had to take was minimal.' In other words, the children were re-visiting the idea of investigating a packet of sweets, and there was very little difference between the two contexts in terms of the materials used. Certainly, the material similarities between the two contexts could be seen as minimizing the 'risk' for the children, although there had been a time lapse of some five weeks between the children's first experience of investigating Smarties and the second investigation with wine gums.

At the same time, Claire recalled, 'I did ask them to record something, but I didn't say what, and I didn't say how. I just said, "Here's some paper. I do want you to record what you do, but you decide how." ' In other words, she withdrew direct instruction or guidance at this point and required the children to work on their own, making decisions about what to do and how to represent their findings. In this way, and contrary to Claire's earlier belief, the open-ended nature of the presentation of the task may have felt quite risky for some of the children. Nevertheless, implicit in Claire's action is an assumption that if children are to use and apply their mathematics knowledge they need to be given opportunities to do so without teacher intervention. Claire emphasized that encouraging children to take risks was part of the shared ethos and practice of the teachers at her school. According to Claire, the teachers played down the idea that there is only one correct way to do things, particularly in mathematics, preferring children to 'have a go'.

Claire felt confident that all the children in her class had enjoyed some success with the wine gums investigation but at varying levels of sophistication. Some children estimated the number in the packet, some counted all the wine gums, some counted one colour only and some were able to generate number sentences such as, 'There are five red and six orange therefore there are eleven altogether.' Similarly, all the children were successful in sharing the wine gums equitably. However, some started by taking random handfuls, compared how many they each had and negotiated changes, whereas other children distributed the sweets one at a time around the group. It seems then, that the children's success could be attributed not only to the lack of risk involved, but also to the fact that embedded within the activity were several equally acceptable successful application outcomes.

Claire's case of unsuccessful application: making a winter picture

Claire's example of unsuccessful application arose from working with a large group (21) of 5- and 6-year-olds on finding different combinations of colours. The class were creating a 'winter picture' and were only able to use red, yellow and blue pens to colour the outfits of the children they had drawn (jumper, trousers, hat). Claire's aim was for the children to work individually (although seated together in small groups) and to generate different colour combinations.

Claire wanted the children to apply their knowledge of 'sameness' and 'difference', identified as key ideas in the early activities recommended in the published mathematics scheme used by her school. She felt that the children were secure in their knowledge of 'the same as', as evidenced by the production of a Noah's Ark picture where the children were responsible for producing pairs of animals. The new task would help Claire check the children's understanding of 'difference' and she was sure that most of the children would succeed.

Claire introduced the task by providing an example of a child dressed in blue jumper, yellow trousers and red hat:

We're going to do a picture and we're going to think of three colours. We're going to use the three primary colours and we're going to see how many *different* sets of clothing we can find. We're going to do caps or hats, we're going to do jumpers and we're going to do trousers and we're going to use three colours: blue, red and yellow. Everybody's going to put a hat on their person and everybody's going to put a jumper on and everybody's going to put a pair of trousers on and they can be either red or blue or yellow.

Claire drew the children's attention to the colours she had used for her example:

Claire: What colour is the hat that I've done?
Children: Red.
Claire: What colour is the jumper?
Children: Blue.
Claire: What colour are the trousers?
Children: Yellow!

The children assured Claire that they knew what they were doing. She repeated the task and asked individual children to say which colours they would use for which items. As the children shared their plans, Claire took the opportunity to highlight where their colour suggestions differed from her example:

Claire: We're all going to see if we can do a different one and you can only use these three colours but we're all going to try and make ours different. What colour will you do your jumper Darren?
Darren: Blue.
Claire: Oh that's the same as mine. What colour will you do yours Sally?
Sally: Red.
Claire: Oh good, yours will be different won't it?

At the outset, the children were convinced that they wouldn't all be able to find a different combination; that is, 21 different combinations of colours. 'No, no we won't, there's too many of us.' In the event, 16 children made exact copies of Claire's model. Three further combinations were generated; one from an individual child, and the other two from two pairs of children sitting next to each other. In other words, four out of the six possible colour combinations were produced among the class, but only five children realized they might differ from the teacher's example.

The outcome of the lesson surprised Claire. 'It must have been my presentation of the task which was confusing.' Yet her introductory discussion of the task had provided the children with all the information they needed to complete it successfully. The initial animation, involvement and contributions offered by the children in the opening discussion were not evident in the final outcomes. Claire's explanation of this disparity centred on young children's tentativeness when engaging with something 'different' coupled with their need to be 'right', resulting in a reluctance to take risks on paper. She also postulated group size and access to the teacher as possible reasons for the children's lack of success:

> Because, when we came to do it in small groups and I was there and they could say, 'Shall I do it blue?' and I'd say 'Well are they the same?' and they would say 'No' and then they'd do it. They just needed somebody there with them. I just had too many in a group altogether.

Kathy's case of successful application: the shelving problem

Kathy's case study of a successful application arose from what she termed an 'authentic' problem, which she had presented to two pupils in her Year 5 class of 9- and 10-year-olds. The children's problem involved calculating the size and number of shelving bays needed by the school to store science resources. Some mathematics shelving was already in place and provided a model for sizing, although the actual space for the science resources had to be created by rearranging other storage items. In order to solve the problem the children would need to identify and combine certain measurements.

Kathy expected the children to use and apply their skills of measuring and their knowledge of addition and division. She also expected them to devise their own strategies for completing and recording the task. The children were required to record their work in a way that gave the head-teacher access to all the information necessary to order the shelving.

Kathy provided the following account of what happened.

> The children planned the task meticulously, drawing a plan of the area. They measured the available wall lengths and found the total. They then measured the width of the existing maths shelving bays and decided to 'allow a bit extra for breathing space'. They estimated that four bays would be a possibility, and one mentally calculated that their total width would be 364 cm. This suggested that there might be room for another bay, but when they calculated they found this exceeded the measured space by 6 cm. They decided to re-measure to see if another 6 cm could be found, and decided that by reducing the 'breathing space', five bays could be accommodated. They returned to me to explain what they had done. I sent them to ask the resources assistant to phone (the suppliers) for a price based on their measurements.

In her discussion of the case study, Kathy said that she viewed 'authentic' activity as activity whereby the children need to know the answer for a reason: 'The problem needs to be answered and the teacher hasn't got the answer neatly stored away somewhere.' Her perspective was exemplified in the shelving problem she had set. The children had a clear purpose in mind: to provide the headteacher with all the information he would need to complete an order for the shelving.

Kathy's case of unsuccessful application: the windows problem

For her example of unsuccessful application, Kathy described a self-initiated task undertaken by one of her Year 5 children. The children had recently been considering evidence about Victorian schools, and they had noted that the classrooms were often very dark. Dean wanted to investigate how large one window would have to be in his classroom in order to let in the same amount of light as the eight windows already present in the room.

Kathy expected Dean to use his knowledge of linear measurement and concept of area to help him solve the problem. She expected him to measure reasonably accurately using standard measures and thought he might possibly use a calculator at some stage. Kathy pointed out that Dean would need to decide on the operation needed to complete the area calculation. She knew that the previous class teacher had covered all these areas of mathematics with the children.

Dean successfully measured the width of one of the windows (84 cm) with a metre stick. He checked that the width of each of the remaining seven windows was also 84 cm. He then calculated 84 cm $\times$ 8 by using repeated addition:

$$
\begin{array}{r}
84 \\
84 \\
84 \\
84 \\
84 \\
84 \\
84 \\
+ \; \underline{84} \\
\hline
\end{array}
$$

He began by adding the units correctly but then decided to use a calculator. His final answer was 596 cm, because he made a keying-in error. He did not pause to check the discrepancy between his original calculation of the units column (resulting in a 2) and the calculator result (6). Kathy asked Dean whether this would be the only measurement that a builder would need to construct the window and he responded with, 'Oh yes, it goes up too!' Dean measured the heights of the windows and then demonstrated his confusion between area and perimeter by declaring: 'I'm going to add up each of the sides to find how much glass there is in the window.'

Kathy partly explained Dean's lack of successful application by suggesting that Dean did not have a secure enough knowledge base in either multiplication or area. She felt that his use of repeated addition for multiplication suggested he was more secure with addition and that 'he has been reluctant to move on'. At the same time, Kathy noted that Dean was highly motivated by the task (he had set the challenge for himself) and she identified this as a key factor in successful application.

> It was a problem the child had set himself and I always find those interesting, because I think that very often, children, if they are motivated, if they have set their own task, then they can very often apply more knowledge than perhaps they would if it's a problem set by the teacher and they don't actually understand what they are trying to do. So I found that interesting because he was very keen to do it, seemed to know what he wanted to do but it turned out that time and again there seemed to be problems where he either didn't have the knowledge that I thought he had or wasn't using it appropriately.

Kathy felt that part of Dean's difficulty may have arisen from his previous experience of mathematics. She suggested that this had involved working through published scheme based exercises or problems set by the teacher 'with neat little answers'. She felt that the prevailing style of teaching that Dean had previously experienced involved the teacher providing a model for completing specific mathematics text exercises and the children completing follow-up practice pages. According to Kathy, this approach to teaching had provided little scope for the children to 'move on to apply their knowledge on their own . . . they are not really asking themselves the right questions, just trying to copy the model the teacher has given them'.

Kathy defined application as 'using mathematics as a tool to serve your purposes wherever you are and whatever you are doing'. She expressed her own conviction that in order for children to be able to apply mathematics, the teacher has to provide them with application strategies. For example, 'helping them to find their way through a problem, breaking it down, what information do you need, helping to talk them through it – I mean getting them to talk me through it because I think that very often it's through getting the child to talk that they are then able to sort out their ideas.'

We don't know from the case study material whether Dean consciously or systematically employed any application strategies to help him solve the problem he had set himself. There is limited evidence that he approached the problem in stages; firstly measuring the window and then making some calculations. However he only reviewed his initial results after Kathy had queried whether the builder would have sufficient measurements to build the window. Dean's final results were in fact based on perimeter as opposed to area measurements, but he was still satisfied with the final outcome. 'He certainly thought that he'd found an answer that was quite satisfactory. He'd done something – measured one of the windows, he'd thought, "Yes, there are eight", done some sort of measurement with all of them, added it up and that was good enough.'

Claire and Kathy: compared and contrasted

There are some common features as well as some differences in the case studies provided by Claire and Kathy. In this section, we look more closely at these similarities and differences, using the questions listed on page 39.

What is the nature of the activities?

Both Claire and Kathy chose activities that had a clear practical nature; that is, they involved the children in using and handling physical materials. As we saw earlier, they were similar in this respect to most of the other teachers in the group, as well as to many of the teachers studied by Askew *et al.* (1993). However, there were differences between Claire and Kathy in the kind of activities they chose. Claire used practical materials as a starting point for the children to explore mathematical ideas and vocabulary in a relatively open-ended way. In contrast, Kathy's practical examples involved the children solving 'real-world' problems, where there was a clearly identifiable purpose for the activity. In this way, Kathy reflected another of Askew's findings, in that applications work was often linked to 'relevant' or 'real-world' activities.

How were these activities meant to promote application?

For both Claire and Kathy, the activities they chose were intended to provide opportunities for children to apply their existing mathematical knowledge to a new situation. Moreover, both teachers were able to articulate in advance the kinds of mathematical knowledge they expected the children to apply. In the wine gums activity, for example, Claire intended the children to apply their knowledge of counting, sorting, sharing and recording. Similarly, in the shelving problem, Kathy expected the children to apply their knowledge of addition, division and measurement. In this respect, the case studies provide a contrast to Askew's finding that, on the whole, the mathematics of the practical activities was not discussed by the teachers or the children.

Askew also found that the teachers' planning did not give specific attention to the processes involved in using and applying mathematics. In contrast, both Claire and Kathy saw their activities as providing opportunities for the children to use some of the process skills that they considered important for application. For example, Claire's introduction to the Smarties investigation suggested that the children might engage in processes such as making decisions about what to do, asking questions, estimating, checking answers and recording their work. Similarly, Kathy's comments on Dean's lack of success with the window problem revealed the importance she attached to application strategies such as asking the right question, finding a way through a problem and checking the results.

What 'theories of application' were held by the two teachers?

By 'theories of application' we mean the beliefs and ideas that teachers have about the way in which application takes place and how it can be fostered in the classroom. While we were not on this occasion able to explore the teachers' beliefs in depth, the case studies still provide some insights into their theories of application.

In Claire's thinking about application, the notion of 'risk' seemed to be of central importance. She believed that applying existing knowledge to a novel situation involved a certain degree of risk, and that this needed to be worked through if children were to be successful in their application. Although she did not use the term herself, Claire thus seemed to believe that 'confidence' was an important ingredient for successful application.

Ideas of confidence and security could also be seen in Kathy's thinking about application. For example, she suggested that Dean's failure to apply his knowledge of multiplication and area might be due to his 'lack of a secure knowledge base' in these areas, and his 'reluctance to move on'. However, she clearly believed that such reluctance could be overcome by providing the children with 'authentic' real-life problems, where there was a genuine purpose for the activity. She felt that such problems – particularly if they were chosen by the children themselves – would generate high levels of motivation, and these high levels of motivation would aid application. At the same time, she also believed that successful application depended on children possessing a number of application strategies, and that it was her role as a teacher to provide children with those strategies.

What did the teachers actually do to promote application?

As we saw above Claire considered 'confidence' to be an important part of application. In practice, she did a number of things to reduce the risk of novel activities for the children and boost their confidence. Thus, in the Smarties investigation she herself modelled the kinds of processes she wanted the children to adopt, while in the wine gums activity she deliberately minimized the difference between this and the previous activity. In the winter picture activity she was again encouraging the children to take risks and choose a colour combination that was different from hers. On this occasion, however, she was not successful, and the children stuck to the security of copying her model.

While Kathy also stressed the importance of confidence, she also believed it was part of her role to teach application strategies explicitly. However, the direct teaching of such strategies was not particularly evident in her case studies. In both the examples she provided, Kathy – like Claire – maintained a low profile once the activities had been introduced, and the children were encouraged to work on the problems for themselves. In this way, it could be argued, the children were really challenged to use and apply their mathematical knowledge.

What opportunities did the activity present for developing process skills?

Our interest here is in the extent to which the case study activities were designed to encourage the process skills of decision making, communicating about mathematics and reasoning. As we saw in Chapter 2, these process skills were integral to the 'using and applying' attainment target in the National Curriculum, and can be identified within the 'solving problems' strand of the Numeracy Framework. We are also interested in whether opportunities arose during the activities for developing these process skills, and whether these opportunities were taken up by the teachers.

Decision making

As we have seen, all the case study activities provided opportunities for the children to engage in practical problem solving. In addition, they all required the children to make decisions about how to approach the task and which mathematics to use. At the same time, there were differences in the level of constraint on the children's decision making imposed by each activity. In the shelving problem, the actual physical space available for the shelves provided some genuine (and helpful) constraints on the choices available to the children. Similarly, restricting the number of colours to be used in the winter picture to three (red, yellow and blue) meant there would be a manageable number of possible combinations for the children to identify. The most 'open' activity was the wine gums investigation, which provided a range of application possibilities and allowed the children to have some success at differing levels of sophistication. In this instance the open-ended nature of the activity did not seem to overwhelm the children. At the same time, the lack of constraints on decision making meant that children could 'play safe' and go for the 'obvious' rather than explore the full range of possibilities.

The activities also presented the children with opportunities to monitor their decision making and reflect on the outcomes this had generated. In some cases, these opportunities were taken, but in others they were not. In the shelving problem, for example, the children decided to 'allow a bit extra for breathing space', but found this only resulted in four shelving bays. They therefore readjusted their earlier decision and found they could now accommodate five bays. In contrast, although the windows problem presented Dean with plenty of opportunities for monitoring his decisions, he did not monitor his work by using checking strategies or stopping to consider the reasonableness of his results.

Communicating about mathematics

All the case study activities provided opportunities for the children to explain their thinking to other people and to consider ways of presenting their results. However, these aspects of application were particularly prominent in the activities chosen by Kathy. Both the shelving and windows problems provided a 'natural' audience to help shape the children's presentation of their information and results. In the shelving problem, the headteacher needed a clear specification of the materials that had to be ordered: similarly, any builder would need accurate measurements to solve the windows problem. In this way, the real-world nature of the problems gave a genuine communicative purpose to the children's recording.

In contrast, the need for the children to record their investigations was not so well defined in Claire's examples. In the case of the winter picture activity, the fact that the mathematics was linked to an art display may have served to confuse the issue, as the boundaries between recording for a classroom display and recording the outcomes of a permutations investigation were necessarily blurred. In the case of the wine gums investigation, the children were not required by Claire to record in any particular way, and so the children were really given scope to present their work in their own way; the only constraints were in relation to whatever mathematics the children decided to investigate.

Reasoning

The case study activities provided relatively few opportunities for mathematical reasoning. For example, there is little evidence of mathematical thinking or reasoning in the wine gums investigation, with the notable exception of Tony (see p. 40). Having shared some of the sweets out (three each) the children were faced with the problem of what to do with the remaining five. Tony persuaded the other three children that there would be enough for one more each by reasoning, 'There's five and four of us'.

There was some evidence in the case studies of children being challenged to explain their thinking and working. For example, in her introduction to the winter picture activity, Claire asked the children how they knew their colour combination was the same as or different from her exemplar. We have also seen how Kathy expected the children to write the shelving specification in a way that explained to the headteacher what materials needed to be ordered and why. Certainly, the shelving problem implicitly involved some 'what if' questions for the children to ask, such as, 'What if each bay measures x?', or 'What if we reduce the breathing space between bays?' Nevertheless, the fact that the case studies centred on practical activity seemed to inhibit the opportunity for the higher order reasoning skills of making generalizations and developing logical proofs.

Overview

Asking the project teachers to provide case studies of successful and unsuccessful application turned out to be a very useful activity. It provided the teachers with an opportunity to reflect on and evaluate their own practice, and to compare their approaches with those of other teachers within the group. At the same time, it provided us with some insights into their initial thinking about application.

The case studies provided by the teachers suggested that their thinking about application was closer to the intentions behind the 'using and applying' attainment target than that of the teachers studied by Askew *et al.* (1993). While there were some similarities between the two studies – in that practical and 'real-life' activities tended to predominate – there were some important differences too. Unlike the teachers in Askew's study, our project teachers were able to specify quite clearly the kind of mathematics they wanted the children to apply. There were also signs that some of them were thinking about application in terms of the process skills of decision making, communication and reasoning. In the next two chapters, we will look at how the teachers' thinking and practice developed from these initial starting points.

Teaching for application at Key Stage 1

In this chapter and the next we will be looking at the ways in which some of the teachers in our project developed their practice in the area of application. As in Chapter 3, these examples are intended to raise some of the central issues involved in teaching for application. At the same time, we indicate where each example might be situated within the Numeracy Framework. Teachers attempting to implement the Numeracy Framework in their own classrooms might therefore see these examples as useful starting points.

The examples presented in this chapter are taken from the project teachers who worked with children at Key Stage 1. In fact, most of these teachers were working with children in Year 1 classes. In the next chapter we will be looking at examples from teachers at Key Stage 2. As we shall see, the issues raised in these two chapters are very similar, despite the difference in the ages of the children.

The examples of practice were obtained in the following way. At an early stage in the project the teachers met as a group with the project team, discussed the aims of the project and shared ideas about application. They also discussed the examples of successful and unsuccessful application that they had provided previously (see Chapter 3). The teachers then went away to develop their thinking about application and put their ideas into practice. The project team did not insist that any particular approach had to be used. The teachers were merely asked to think carefully about how they might help their pupils apply mathematical knowledge, to implement their ideas in a systematic way, and reflect on the success or otherwise of the approach adopted.

During this period, each teacher was observed carrying out a lesson in their classroom. Supply cover was made available if any of the teachers wanted to work with a small group, or take time out to set up an activity. Before each lesson, the teachers filled out a questionnaire in which they set out what they intended to do and why. During the lesson, tape-recordings were made of classroom interaction, and samples of the children's work were taken away for analysis. After the lesson, the teachers were interviewed about how they felt the lesson had gone. On occasion, some of the children were also interviewed during or after the lesson to elicit their perceptions of what they had done and why they had done it. The teachers then met again with the project team to discuss what they were doing and to develop their ideas about application. As before, they then went away to put their ideas into practice. This cycle – discussion, experimentation and further discussion – was repeated several times in the course of the project.

In this chapter, each example of practice will first be presented as a straightforward narrative account. Each narrative will then be followed by a short commentary. The commentary will be based around the questions introduced in Chapter 3:

- What is the nature of the activity?
- How is it intended to promote application?
- What is the teacher's theory of application?
- What does the teacher actually do to promote application?
- What opportunities does the activity present for developing the process skills of decision making, communicating about mathematics and reasoning?

Alice and the car boot sale

Alice taught a Year 1 class of 5- and 6-year-old children. In the following example, she wanted the children to apply their existing mathematical knowledge in a 'real-life' context that they might encounter outside the classroom. Alice decided to make the context as realistic as possible by setting up a 'car boot sale' in the classroom, in which the children had to buy and sell goods using real money. She chose this activity as she wanted to create a situation in which the children would need to apply their existing knowledge of addition and (particularly) subtraction. As she explained:

> It's an authentic activity. Where would children use subtraction in real life? When adding on isn't the most appropriate operation to use? Subtraction is a National Curriculum requirement and I see it as a legitimate activity. Creating a car boot sale in class is where they can apply their understanding.

Before the lesson, Alice said she had two main aims for the activity. Firstly, she wanted to 'help the children acquire a strategy or technique to see if they are able to select the correct process of subtraction and apply it'. Secondly, she was trying to 'develop a secure knowledge base with young children, using small numbers, so that higher numbers can then be used, to counter the automatic strategy of adding on'. Alice also felt that an important part of the activity was that the children would work in small groups. She wanted the children to be responsible to the group rather than to her, adding that she was 'not sure if application takes place if under the direct control of the teacher'.

Alice prepared for the car boot sale over several lessons. She used pretend money in the home corner, and took some of the children to a real shop to purchase goods and work out the change. On the day before the car boot sale, she did some work with her class on addition and subtraction involving money, explicitly linking this to the following day's activity.

On the day of the sale itself, Alice gave the children some practice in using subtraction as a means of calculating change. She drew a cake on a sheet of paper and told the children that it cost 5p. She suggested that they imagine they were selling the cake, and asked how much change they would give if someone gave them 50p. Several children replied '45p'. One child, Hayley, explained that she had done this by 'counting back – 49, 48, 47, 46, 45'.

Alice then drew a bigger cake with lots of candles on it, and told the children this cake cost 15p. As before, she asked them how much change they would give for 50p. Again, many children seemed to be counting back from 50p. However, one child, Ruth, explained that 'I had 50p and I took 10p away which gave me 40, and I took 5 away and I was left with 35'.

Alice then introduced the car boot sale. The children had brought in a range of articles from home that were no longer wanted and that they were going to 'sell' to their classmates. Alice organized them into four groups, and gave each group £2.00 (in real currency) to spend at the sale. The children priced the goods themselves, although Alice suggested that no item should be more than 5p. She told them they would need to develop their own ways of keeping track of the money. At the end of the day they would have to account for all their exchanges.

The first part of the activity involved each group in setting up its stall, pricing their goods, and devising a method for keeping track of the money. Alice took a few children aside and modelled what might take place later on:

Alice: Let's have a little practice, shall we? I'll pretend I'm coming to buy something. Now I've got 5p and I'd like to buy this book which is 4p. How much change will you give me?
Peter: 1p.

The sale started, with the children taking turns to be buyers and sellers.

Most of the children seemed to have understood what they were being asked to do, and appeared to be calculating the change correctly. For example:

> (Mickey picks up a car on the stall)
> *Carl:*   Is that 5p?
> *Mickey:* No, 3p. And I've got 5p.
> *Carl:*   There (opens till and gives 2p change).

The children devised some interesting methods for keeping track of their money. One child, for example, represented on paper each item he had sold as a number with a circle around it. He was able to use this system later to check that his actual takings were correct. Another group of children devised a system that resembled an old-fashioned ledger, with outgoings on one side and incomings on the other (see Figure 4.1). One child explained the system as follows: 'What you do is, you write down what people have been selling [points to the left-hand column] and you count up the prices and that one's the things that you bought' [points to right hand column].

At the end of the sale Alice asked each group of children to add up their money and see if they had ended with more or less than they started with.

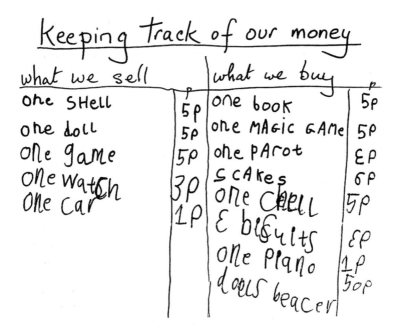

Figure 4.1   Recording transactions in the car boot sale

She then brought all the children together and explained that as they had started the day with £8.00 altogether, they should end the day with the same amount. However, when the children added together what each group had left, the total came to £7.93. It seemed that 7p had mysteriously disappeared!

Afterwards, Alice considered that the lesson had gone very well. She felt that the activity had been 'exciting' for the children, and that 'it had made their use of mathematics in general much more important'. As a result, they had carried out their calculations much more rapidly than they would normally have done.

> They applied subtraction probably more than I expected them to. And I was really pleased with that, for it was a much more efficient way of dealing with some of those transactions. And I thought they were certainly applying it a lot of the time, with the lower numbers as well, with the change, and I found that was interesting, because before with lower numbers they immediately added on. So they actually now have a wider range to call on.

Alice also commented on her own role in the activity, and in particular on the way she had tried to model various strategies for the children.

> I think adult intervention is quite important. I think children should think for themselves, but I also think that learning is much more efficient if they are shown certain techniques sometimes, or have a model of something that is going to work. And I feel it is much better for them to see something, and either use it or adapt it for their own use, rather than to struggle for a long time, and then come to something that you have in your mind later on. That's how I tend to work.

The car boot sale: a commentary

The car boot sale is an example of a practical, 'real-life' activity involving money calculations. Within the Numeracy Framework, such an activity might be used to meet the objective that 'pupils should be taught to . . . solve simple word problems involving money and explain how the problem was solved' (DfEE 1999, section 5: 68), although the car boot sale feels somewhat different from many of the word problems found in the Numeracy Framework (see p. 34). The Numeracy Framework also suggests that Year 1 pupils might 'use their own mental strategies to solve problems involving money in contexts such as the classroom shop' (p. 68). In the car boot sale, Alice's purpose was to provide an opportunity for the children to apply their knowledge of addition and (particularly) subtraction. She also wanted the children to devise their own methods for keeping track of the money exchanges. In both these respects, Alice considered the activity a success.

The example provides some insights into Alice's theory of application.

She considered that she was providing an 'authentic' activity, and that this would make the mathematics more 'exciting' and 'important'. She believed that increasing the children's motivation in this way would lead to more extensive and rapid application of their existing knowledge. However, there appeared to be some confusion in Alice's views about her own role in application. Before the lesson she had commented that she was 'not sure if application takes place if under the direct control of the teacher', whereas after the lesson she remarked that 'learning is much more efficient if they are shown certain techniques sometimes, or have a model of something that is going to work'. Certainly, she seemed to take a more directive role during the lesson itself, giving the children exercises in subtraction and modelling its use before the sale got under way.

The car boot sale appeared to provide plenty of opportunities for developing the process skills of decision making, communication and reasoning. Much of the discussion that took place between the children involved communication about mathematics; for example, when fixing prices or calculating change. In particular, asking the children to devise a method for recording their transactions gave a good deal of scope for reasoning about numbers and explaining their methods to other children. Moreover, Alice was able to draw the children's attention to the underlying mathematical logic of the sale – that they should end with the same amount of money that they started with – even though in reality 7p had gone missing! At the same time, Alice's emphasis on the children using subtraction seemed to inhibit the possibility of the children themselves deciding which method – counting, counting-on or subtraction – was the most appropriate for any particular calculation. In other words, there seemed to be a conflict between Alice's desire that the children should use one particular operation, and giving children opportunities to decide for themselves which mathematics they should use and apply.

Fiona and the teddy drive game

Several of the project teachers used mathematical games as part of their approach to application. This was particularly so among the teachers who were working at Key Stage 1. Indeed, one of these teachers, Fiona, used games throughout the project as her preferred method for promoting application.

At an early stage in the project, Fiona devised a game for her Year 1–2 children that was very similar to the well known 'beetle drive' game. Each child was given a sheet of paper divided into four. In the top left-hand corner of each sheet Fiona had drawn a picture of a teddy bear (see Figs 4.2 and 4.3). Underneath the teddy she had written the values attached to each part of the teddy's anatomy. Thus the body scored four, the head scored three, the ears two each, and the arms and legs one each.

Fiona intended that the game would help children apply their knowledge of addition. They were able to add small numbers presented in standard written form (for example, 3 + 5 = ?), using concrete materials such as Multi-link to help them. However, they had little experience of adding more than two numbers at once. Fiona predicted that 'the children will be well motivated to want to add their scores and will find a way of doing this, either by writing, drawing or using Multi-link'.

During the case study, Fiona worked with two groups of three children. She started by explaining that the aim was to draw a teddy. The children were to take it in turns to throw the dice, but they could not start on their drawings until they had thrown a four for the body. Once they had drawn a body they could add a head with a throw of three, and a leg or arm with a throw of one. She said they could draw an ear with a throw of two, even if they hadn't yet got a head. The first child to draw a complete teddy was to shout 'Teddy!', and at that point everyone else had to stop and add up

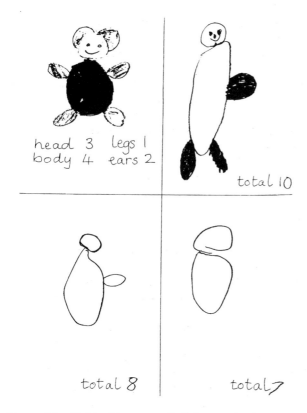

Figure 4.2   Teddy drive game: Celia's scoresheet

their score. Fiona explained that the one who shouted 'Teddy!' would have a score of 15, and continued:

Fiona: If you haven't got them all you have to somehow work out how much you've got to put here. You can use anything you like to work it out with, right? You could use Multi-link. What else could you use?

Jody: Calculator.

Fiona: Would you be happy using the calculator to find out? Would it be easier to use the Multi-link, do you think?

Celia: Harder.

Ryan: Easier.

Fiona: Shall we see? Shall we find out?

The game started and the children were soon heavily engaged with it. They helped each other out, calling out comments like 'Two is an ear!' Fiona moved from one table to another, observing what they were doing and providing help when required. One child, Douglas, completed his teddy and shouted 'Teddy!' Fiona asked the other children to stop and add up their scores. Most seemed able to do this, with varying degrees of assistance from the teacher.

Celia, for example, had little trouble in mentally calculating her score. Her teddy had a body, a head, an arm and two legs (see Figure 4.2):

Celia: I've got ten.

Fiona: How do you know you've got ten?

Celia: Look (points to the body) – four.
(Points to the head) five, six, seven.
(Points to each arm and leg) eight, nine, ten.

Fiona: Four for the body, five, six, seven . . . eight, nine, ten . . . right.

Unlike Celia, Jody needed some help from Fiona in adding up his score. His teddy had a body, a head, an ear and a leg (see Figure 4.3).

Fiona: Here we are. Look. What have you got? You've got a body which is four, a head is three . . .

Jody: What's an ear?

Fiona: Two. So a body is four, and a head is three, what's that?

Jody: Seven.

Fiona: Then you've got two for an ear.

Jody: Nine.

Fiona: Right. Then you've got a leg.

Jody: Ten.

Fiona: Ten. Yes, right. You've got ten haven't you?

Jody: Ten (writes this down on paper). A one and a nought.

A third child, Ryan, was having considerable difficulty adding up his score. His teddy had a body, a head, two ears and two legs. He tried to use

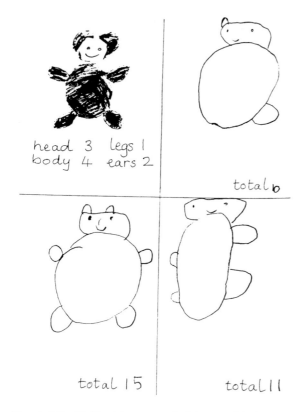

head 3   legs 1
body 4   ears 2

total 6

total 15   total 11

Figure 4.3   Teddy drive game: Jody's scoresheet

his fingers to add up the score, but was unsuccessful. He then tried to use Multi-link. He put four Multi-link cubes on the body, three on the head, and one on each leg, but only one on each ear. Despite Fiona's intervention, he found it hard to realize that he needed two Multi-link on each ear. He seemed confused by the whole situation and had difficulty adding up the Multi-link to obtain an overall score.

The game continued for a further two rounds. At the end, the children used the calculator to add up their scores from the three games. Fiona obtained the total scores from each group and wrote them on the board. She ended the lesson by asking the children to identify the biggest and smallest totals, and to say who had scored the most and the least.

Afterwards, Fiona said she was very pleased with how the lesson had gone. She felt that most of the children had succeeded in what she wanted them to do, and that in large part this had been due to the motivating power of the game.

> I think playing a game together like that is a good motivating way to give . . . they see a reason for adding those numbers up. If I had said to them we were going to add these numbers together now, they would not have seen any point to it. They would probably have found it a lot more difficult.

Fiona commented on the children who had experienced difficulty in their calculations. She pointed out the confusion several children had felt in remembering the value of the head, legs and ears. She noted that they had tended to count each limb as 'one' rather than the value it had been given. She felt that Jody had grasped what was required as the session had progressed. In contrast, she felt that Ryan had struggled throughout:

> He didn't know how to go about it, he didn't apply. He was totally floored by how he was going to get his total score. He just said, 'I can't do it.' It was almost a mental blockage, that he was frightened, he was frightened to try anything. And it prevented him from thinking about what we frequently use; Multi-links or add up. He has not had so many numbers to add up before so obviously it was rather scary for him.

Teddy drive: a commentary

In this example, Fiona designed a mathematical game involving dice for the children in her Year 1–2 class. In terms of the Numeracy Framework, the game might be seen as providing an opportunity for pupils to *'choose and use appropriate number operations and ways of calculating to solve problems'* (DfEE 1999, section 5: 60). In this case, the game was intended to help children apply their knowledge of addition, by providing a context in which they were required to add together two or more numbers. In this respect, Fiona thought the activity had been successful. Like Alice in the previous example, she judged the success of the activity primarily in terms of whether or not the children used a particular mathematical operation.

In Fiona's theory of application, the children's emotional state appeared to play a central role. She attributed the success of the activity to the motivating properties of the game, saying that if the additions had been presented outside the game context, then the children would have been less likely to apply their knowledge. Fiona also attributed the difficulties experienced by Ryan to his emotional state. According to Fiona, Ryan's fear had overwhelmed any positive motivation from playing the game, and had led to him developing a 'mental blockage', which effectively prevented him from using his existing mathematical knowledge. As a corollary to this, Fiona made few references to her own possible role in facilitating application. In this respect, her practice appeared to follow her theory, as her main role during the game was limited to checking the children's calculations and helping those who were experiencing difficulties.

The teddy drive game essentially provided a context in which the children could practise and extend their skills of addition. In terms of the process skills of decision making, communication and reasoning, it seemed to be of limited value. True, the children had to make decisions about the methods they would use to carry out the additions; there was also some discussion about the values of different parts of the teddy's body. However, the game provided no real choice about which number operation should be used, and few opportunities for genuine mathematical communication or reasoning.

Barbara and writing number stories

Barbara had recently moved to become deputy head and mathematics co-ordinator of a new school. She felt that mathematics teaching in the school had been dominated for some time by the use of commercial mathematics schemes. She thought that the children were quite competent at dealing with problems when presented in the standard format in their workbooks. However, she thought they had a very limited understanding of what these standard representations meant.

Before one lesson, Barbara wrote that she intended to 'provide a meaningful context for children to enable them to see how algorithms relate to "real life" and to see if they can provide "stories" for algorithms'. Barbara intended to preface this with a discussion in which she would ask the children why they were learning mathematics, raising questions such as 'Is it useful?' and 'When might we need maths?' She wanted the children to work in pairs 'because I suspect they've never been called upon to "talk" about maths before and they need to be collaborative, at least in pairs'. Barbara thought this activity would be totally new for the children, saying that 'maths has always been working in books for them'.

The lesson proceeded as Barbara had outlined. She started by asking the children why they were learning to read. The children gave a number of answers that suggested they understood that they were acquiring a skill that might prove useful in other contexts; for example, they might need to read instructions, or the words in a song book. Barbara then asked them why they were learning mathematics. This time it proved harder to elicit suggestions from the children, but with some persistence ideas started to emerge. For example, it was suggested that a shopkeeper might use mathematics to add up the day's takings, that a teacher would need to know how to add up dinner money, and that a builder would need mathematics to find out how many bricks to put in a house.

Barbara seemed pleased with these responses and moved on to the next part of her lesson. She wrote the following sum on a flipchart:

$$
\begin{array}{r}
12 \\
+\ \ 7 \\
\hline
19
\end{array}
$$

and asked the children to 'tell me a story about that sum'. As before, the children found it hard to know how to respond. Eventually, Philip suggested, 'there were 12 caterpillars on a leaf and seven more came along and that gave 19'.

Barbara wrote another sum on the flipchart:

$$
\begin{array}{r}
20 \\
-\ \ 9 \\
\hline
11
\end{array}
$$

and again asked for 'a story about the sum'. This time Rachel suggested, somewhat bizarrely, 'There were 20 people reading a book and nine went away, and that left 11'. At this point, Barbara provided a 'story' of her own, in which there were 20 people in a cinema and nine left, leaving 11 inside. She attempted to situate this in a meaningful context by suggesting that the cinema doorman would need to know how many people he could now let in.

Barbara then gave each child a clipboard and some paper, and asked them to write some sums, as she had done, and to write underneath 'the story of that sum'. She stressed that the children should 'Think very carefully about real things that might actually happen. It's very important that you try to link it to something that might really happen. If you can't then make up a story which is close to that.'

The children settled down to produce their sums and stories. For the most part they stuck to additions and subtractions up to 30. Many of their stories involved animals, food or sporting activities. Rachel, for example, produced an addition involving cats and kittens, a subtraction in which ten rabbits were shot, and another addition involving people and their friends (see Figure 4.4). Another child, Charlie, produced a subtraction story involving ten-pin bowling, another subtraction involving apples being shaken from a tree, and an addition story about a boy called Charlie scoring 11 goals in the first half a football match and 12 in the second (see Figure 4.5). Barbara moved around the class, discussing the stories with the children. At the end of the lesson, she asked some of the children to explain their stories to the whole class.

After the lesson, Barbara reflected on how it had gone. She said she had been trying to get the children to see some kind of relevance to school mathematics, and to make some kind of connection between what they did in their mathematics books and 'real life'. She felt that some of the children had started to make some connections, 'but it took quite a while for the penny to drop'. She noted that when she asked them to think of situations where mathematics might be useful, their main response was to

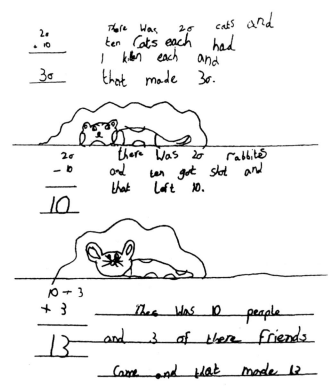

$$\begin{array}{r} 2\sigma \\ +\ 10 \\ \hline 30 \end{array}$$

There Was 20 cats and ten Cats each had 1 kiten each and that made 30.

$$\begin{array}{r} 2\sigma \\ -\ 6 \\ \hline 10 \end{array}$$

there Was 20 rabbits and ten got shot and that Left 10.

$$\begin{array}{r} 10 + 3 \\ +\ 3 \\ \hline 13 \end{array}$$

Thee Was 10 people and 3 of there Friends Come and that made 13

Figure 4.4   Rachel's stories

think in terms of money, 'which does seem to be very relevant to them; they can see the sense of needing to know about addition and subtraction of money'. She also commented, 'I was trying to work from what we do in school and all the different activities we do in school, and why are we in school? I mean, I don't think we ask ourselves things like that very often'.

Barbara was somewhat disappointed in the stories the children had written, commenting that most of them simply reproduced the kind of 'twee' story they encountered in their mathematics schemes. She commented positively on Charlie's stories, saying that he was beginning to see how one might need mathematics in the real world, and that he was 'making realistic connections'. In contrast, she was more critical of Rachel's work, suggesting that her stories were very typical of those that might be found in mathematics schemes. She considered that Rachel 'hadn't allowed herself to move away from that'.

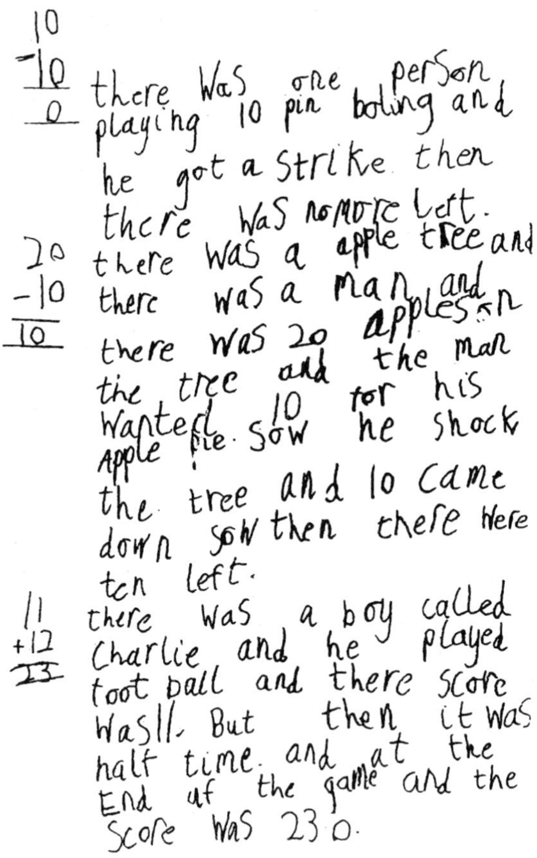

```
 10
-10    there was one person
  0    playing 10 pin boling and
       he got a strike then
       there was nomore Left.
 20    there was a apple tree and
-10    there was a man and
 10    there was 20 apples an
       the tree and the man
       the tree  10 for his
       wanted. pie. sow he shock
       apple
       the tree and 10 came
       down sow then these were
       ten left.
 11    there was a boy called
+12    Charlie and he played
 23    foot ball and there score
       was 11. But then it was
       half time. and at the
       End of the game and the
       score was 23 0.
```

Figure 4.5 Charlie's stories

Writing number stories: a commentary

Barbara's approach to application was rather different from that of Alice or Fiona. Rather than getting the children to use a particular mathematical operation, she wanted the children to invent a story that was some kind of 'real-life' enactment of that operation (or 'algorithm' as she somewhat confusedly called it). She wanted the children to make connections between the mathematics they encountered in their mathematics schemes and 'real life', and she judged the success of the activity in terms of how far the children had moved from the kind of examples they encountered in the scheme.

The activity revealed something of Barbara's theory of application. Essentially, she saw it as a process of 'making connections'. She thought that children would not apply the knowledge they had gained in their school mathematics scheme unless they could see how it might be 'useful' or 'relevant' to life outside school. Writing stories and discussing possible uses for mathematics were two ways of helping children make these connections. At the same time, Barbara appeared to think that making connections involved taking some kind of risk, and that children such as Rachel had preferred instead to cling to the security of the mathematics scheme. Because of this, she saw her own role as important, particularly in modelling for the children the kinds of connections she hoped they would make.

Within the Numeracy Framework, making up number stories to reflect mathematical statements is a suggested activity throughout Key Stage 1. In the Numeracy Framework, this activity is presented within the 'solving problems' strand as a means of helping children make decisions about which operation to use when solving problems: it should be noted, however, that the Numeracy Framework does not introduce the vertical layout of sums at this stage. Carrying out the activity in small groups or pairs, as Barbara did, also increases the opportunities for the children to discuss their stories and explain their thinking to each other. In contrast, it is harder to find a place within the Numeracy Framework for Barbara's first activity, in which the children took part in a discussion on 'Why are we learning maths?' And yet, it seems somewhat strange to suggest that such a discussion should not be a fundamental part of any mathematics curriculum. As Barbara herself pointed out, 'I don't think we ask ourselves things like that very often.'

Diane: exploring a sum

Diane taught a Year 1 class of 5- and 6-year-old children. Her thinking about application changed notably during the course of the project. In the early stages, she was trying to get her children to make connections between their existing mathematical knowledge and possible new situations. However, as the project developed, she became particularly interested in helping children reflect more deeply on their current mathematical understanding.

In the first lesson we observed, Diane's approach was very similar to that of Barbara. She started the lesson with a discussion about how mathematics might be used in 'real life'. During this discussion, she told the children how she had used mathematics herself in planning the lesson; for example, in working out how many chairs and tables she would need in the classroom. Next, she wrote on a flipchart some addition and subtraction sums, and asked the children to write number stories about them. Like Barbara, she found it harder than she had expected to elicit suitable responses from the children.

Afterwards, Diane reflected on why this might be. She explained that in a previous activity the children had found it easy to extract the mathematics from a story, so she had expected them to find it easy to make connections in the opposite direction; from the mathematics to a story. She went on to say that she was starting to rethink her approach to application:

Researcher: What are you trying to do to achieve successful application?

Diane: Well, I thought I was trying to tie it in to real situations, when I gave the example of me working out chairs and that sort of thing, to get them to think about using these number operations in real life. I'm not so sure now!

Researcher: So where will you go from here?

Diane: I'm interested now in narrowing it right down, and perhaps exploring in more depth one number. Really, that might tell me more. Let's see what we can do with just one number.

Researcher: One number sentence?

Diane: I don't know. Maybe it's just possible to look at a number and see . . . that may be the next stage on again, I don't know. Maybe start with one sum. But I would also be interested to see what different stories they could make from a number, or different ways of looking at a number. I must give that more thought.

Later in the project, Diane had the opportunity to put this idea into practice. She spent an intensive session working with two children, Karen and Simon, helping them explore in some depth the meaning of a few number sentences. In her pre-lesson questionnaire, Diane explained the rationale for this activity:

I aim to explore the 'hidden' relationships between the numbers and symbols of a simple algorithm and to encourage the children to articulate their understanding and their actions. I have decided to work with two children only in order to monitor closely the procedures and language employed. This may not be realistic but will at this stage be useful. I intend to initiate a discussion with the children which will aim to explore the *content* of a simple algorithm. The task is to make the number cards and symbols work together. It is new for me as I have not considered the power and content of a simple sum before – at least not to this extent. I expect the children to apply (or not) their knowledge of the functions of +, – and =, and the learnt conventions of sums to a new mathematical content.

Diane started by introducing Karen and Simon to three cards on which she had written +, – and =. She talked to the children about what these symbols meant, reminding them that 'sometimes they have a special job to do when they are in a sum'. She then illustrated these 'jobs' by writing 2 + 3 = 5 on a flipchart, and discussed with them the role that the + and = signs played within this particular number sentence.

Diane then gave each child a set of cards. Each card had either a sign on it or a numeral. Karen's cards were: ②, ⑤, ⑦, ⊞, ⊟, and ⊜. Simon's cards were ③, ⑥, ⑨, ⊞, ⊟, and ⊜. Diane said, 'I want you to just have a look at them and see if you can find different ways to put them all out and make them work together.' Altogether, the children spent about 20 minutes working with their particular set of cards.

Karen found the activity easier than Simon did. For example, she produced ⑦ ⊟ ② ⊜ ⑤ followed by ⑤ ⊞ ② ⊜ ⑦. When questioned by Diane as to what she was doing, Karen replied that she was 'putting the answer at the beginning' (that is, transferring the 5 from the end of the first sum to the start of the next one). Later, she produced ② ⊞ ⑤ ⊜ ⑦. This led Diane to comment, 'So you've kept the same answer, you've just changed the adding numbers around, OK?'

In contrast, Simon had some difficulty with the activity. He started appropriately enough with ③ ⊞ ⑥ ⊜ ⑨, but then followed it with ③ ⊟ ⑨ ⊜ ⑥. This led to the following conversation.

Diane: Can you tell me what you've done?
Simon: Three take away nine equals six.
Diane: Is that going to work? What do you think now?
(Simon shakes head)
Diane: Do you know why not?
Simon: Because that number [points to the 3] is smaller than nine.
Diane: Ah! The three's smaller than the nine. So do you have to have a big number first?
Karen: (interrupts) I would turn it the other way round, the nine and the three.

Simon followed Karen's suggestion and switched the cards round to read ⑨ ⊟ ③ ⊜ ⑥, However, his next attempt was ⑥ ⊟ ⑨ ⊜ ③.

Diane: OK. Are you happy with that? Does that work out OK? Have another look at it to be sure. You can use your fingers. It's OK, I don't mind seeing them. What do think now?
Simon: I think it doesn't work.
Diane: It doesn't work. Remember you told me something about these two numbers here (points to 6 and 9)? You said something about how big these numbers were?
Simon: Six is smaller than nine.
Diane: So do you want to change anything?
(Simon changes his cards to read ⑨ ⊞ ⑥ ⊜ ③)
Diane: Ah! You've changed the sign as well. Right. Now, nine add six, use my fingers, how many shall I give you?

Simon: (works with his and Diane's fingers) Nine add six equals three.
Diane: Does that sound right?
Simon: No.
Diane: You have another look at that and see if you can find some-
thing you are happy with.

Simon sorted his cards again and ended up with $\boxed{6}$ $\boxed{+}$ $\boxed{3}$ $\boxed{=}$ $\boxed{9}$. At Diane's
suggestion, he checked it with his fingers, and was happy with it. They
then compared this sum with an earlier one he had produced, $\boxed{9}$ $\boxed{-}$ $\boxed{3}$ $\boxed{=}$
$\boxed{6}$.

Diane: What's your six doing in this sum here? What's its job here?
Simon: It's the answer.
Diane: Right. You've got it as the answer in this one, but in this one
here (indicates 6 + 3 = 9) it's adding with the three, isn't it? Its
adding up together to *give* the answer, but here you've moved
it to *be* the answer.

The session ended with some discussion about whether a particular sum
could be turned round, so that the 'answer' was on the left-hand side.
This proved to be a difficult idea for the children to grasp, even for Karen.
She started to put out her cards like this: $\boxed{7}$ $\boxed{=}$ but then said 'It doesn't
work'.

Afterwards, Diane felt the session had been a qualified success. She was
critical of her own role, saying that she hadn't used the kind of language
that she had planned to use. However, she justified her use of terms such
as 'work' and 'job', feeling they were appropriate in this context.

They'd used this kind of language before, you know. 'Oh, that doesn't
work', or, 'This doesn't work there', that kind of thing, so it seemed
fairly logical to say, 'OK, if something's happening in this sum, what
are these bits doing?' It naturally followed on to say, 'So has this got a
job to do?', and, 'What's it doing?', you know, 'What is that job?'

Diane felt pleased with the way the children had explored various combinations and with the way in which they had discussed with her what they
were doing. She was particularly pleased by her decision to focus inten-
sively on one or two number sentences.

I feel they have had a lot of practice, if you like, of simply going
through the procedures I have taught them, but that doesn't necessarily mean they know what is going on. So I feel that one of the ways
might be to get more depth really, to see what is actually happening,
and you probably don't need then a million examples. It might be
better just to kind of limit it, because I keep saying this, I'm amazed
at how much there is going on in one simple algorithm.

Exploring a sum: a commentary

The activity that Diane used to promote application was different again from those of Alice, Fiona and Barbara. Although her activity had a practical nature, in that the children had to manipulate physical objects, these objects were in fact cards showing the numerals and symbols of mathematics. The children's task was to generate sentences using these cards, and the success of the activity was judged by whether or not the sentences 'worked' – that is, represented correct additions or subtractions.

The activity gave some indications as to Diane's theory of application. Like Barbara, she believed that children would not necessarily be able to apply their mathematical knowledge if that knowledge was based on carrying out routine procedures in the classroom. However, unlike Barbara, she believed that children should be taught to reflect on those procedures in order to give them a greater understanding of what they meant. When the children subsequently encountered a novel problem, their deeper understanding of mathematics would allow them to carry out a successful application.

Diane felt the children needed an appropriate language to encourage their reflection. For her, this language involved functional terms such as 'job' and 'work'. During the activity, one of Diane's main roles was to provide this language for the children, by asking questions such as, 'Is that going to work?' and, 'What's its job here?' Another role that Diane filled was to suggest a concrete representation (her own and the children's fingers), which the children could use to check whether particular sums did indeed 'work'.

Diane's activity might be described as an 'investigation within mathematics itself'. It is in fact quite similar to the following example taken from the Numeracy Framework. Here, this activity is presented as a suggestion for encouraging *'reasoning about numbers'* at Year 2:

Use 1, 4 and 5, and the signs +, – and =
What different answers can you make?

(DfEE 1999, section 5: p. 63)

It is not entirely clear from the Numeracy Framework whether this activity should be used in the way that Diane did, or whether it is intended that children should generate a series of sums such as:

$$1 + 4 - 5 = 0$$
$$1 + 5 - 4 = 2$$

and so on.

Diane's example suggests that this activity can be used to introduce and discuss the various functions that symbols are performing in a sum, as well as whether the sum overall does or does not 'work'. In other words, Diane's activity not only provides opportunities for children to reason about number, it also allows them to develop their understanding of the nature of mathematical symbols.

Overview

In this chapter we have presented examples of how four teachers at Key Stage 1 developed their practice in the area of application. We have also provided commentaries on these examples in terms of the nature and purposes of the activities, the teachers' theories and practice concerning application and the opportunities for developing the process skills of decision making, communication and reasoning. In addition, we have indicated where each activity might be situated within the Numeracy Framework. Other teachers may find these examples helpful when attempting to implement the Numeracy Framework in their own classrooms.

Looking across the four examples, one is struck by the diversity within the approaches adopted by the different teachers. Clearly, there was little consensus among the teachers in the kind of activities they thought would encourage application or in their views about how application would best be achieved. At the same time, it was possible to identify some common themes within these contrasting approaches. Both Alice and Fiona, for example, believed that motivation was crucial for application, and both believed that their activities had worked because they provided a clear rationale for the children to apply their knowledge. In the same way, Barbara and Diane shared a belief that children would be unlikely to apply if their knowledge was limited to carrying out routine procedures in the classroom. However, the approaches they adopted to 'activate' the children's knowledge were quite different.

These four examples also raise some fundamental issues about teaching for application in the classroom. For example, the car boot sale raises the question of how far we can go in introducing 'real life' into the classroom, and how far this is desirable. Both the car boot sale and the teddy drive game illustrate the conflict between wanting children to use a particular operation and allowing them to choose between different operations. All four examples show that developing process skills is not easy: they also raise questions about how far and in what ways teachers should intervene to promote application. As we shall see in the next chapter, these issues are by no means restricted to teaching for application at Key Stage 1.

Teaching for application at Key Stage 2

In this chapter we present some further examples of ways in which the project teachers developed their practice in the area of application. Here, all the examples come from teachers who were working at Key Stage 2. As before, these examples are intended to raise issues about teaching for application in the classroom. Where appropriate we also indicate where the examples might be used to meet the objectives of the Numeracy Framework.

What differences might we expect as we move from Key Stage 1 to Key Stage 2? As the children are a few years older, we might expect them to be more advanced in their understanding of mathematics and possess a wider range of strategies for dealing with problems. We might also expect them to have a more extensive 'real-world' knowledge, which they might use, for example, when judging the reasonableness of their solutions. As we shall see in this chapter, these expectations are not necessarily fulfilled.

As in Chapter 4, we will present each example as a narrative account of what happened, followed by a short commentary. As before, we will focus our comments around the following questions:

- What is the nature of the activity?
- How is it intended to promote application?
- What is the teacher's theory of application?
- What does the teacher actually do to promote application?
- What opportunities does the activity present for developing the process skills of decision making, communicating about mathematics and reasoning?

Heather and 'Party time!'

Heather designed an activity called 'Party time!' for her Year 5 class. The activity centred on a party that four imaginary children were organizing for their friends. The activity involved carrying out some of the mathematical calculations that these four children would encounter in the course of organizing their party. All the calculations involved money, and were presented as 'word problems' on the worksheet shown in Figure 5.1.

Before the lesson, Heather wrote that the activity would 'present the children with a real-life situation in which they will need to apply their strategy of using division'. She had recently done some work with the class in which they had used calculators to carry out divisions such as 747 ÷ 3 and 195 ÷ 13. They had also done some divisions on the calculator involving money, such as £79.20 ÷ 18. This had caused some confusion

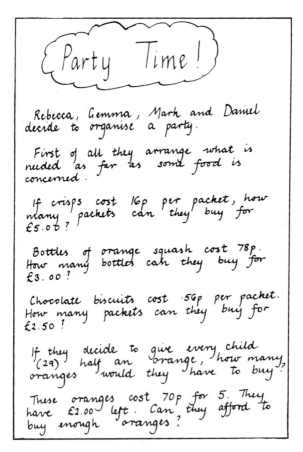

Figure 5.1 'Party time!' worksheet

when the calculator showed 4.4, and the children had discussed whether this meant £4.04 or £4.40. In her pre-lesson questionnaire, Heather wrote, 'In "Party time!" I am expecting children to apply the strategy of using the calculator for division in order to make sense of the food/money requirements.'

Heather considered that the 'Party time!' activity would be an 'authentic example of division'. She intended to 'present the task very simply – they will need to decide how best to organize their approach!' Heather predicted that the children would readily apply their knowledge of division, and that most children would complete the activity 'confidently, quickly and successfully'.

Heather introduced the activity to her class and handed out the worksheets. She suggested that the children work in groups of two or three, and provided each group with paper and a calculator. She did not, however, suggest any specific methods that they might use to solve the problems on the sheet.

The class started work. It soon became apparent that many of the children were not applying their knowledge of division in the manner that Heather intended. Instead, the children were approaching the problems in a number of different ways.

For a start, some children did not interpret the activity as requiring them to use division at all. Instead, these children decided to solve the problems by estimating likely answers. They then checked these by carrying out multiplications on the calculator to see whether they were correct. Thus one group wrote their answer to the second problem as follows:

To get the answer of 3 bottles we done this
3 × 78 = £2.34, which is the nearest to £3.00

Other children did indeed interpret the problems as Heather had intended, and attempted to solve them by using division. These children, however, were confused about exactly what they were dividing by what. Ceri and Marilyn, for example solved the first problem by entering 16 ÷ 5 on the calculator. On obtaining an answer of 3.2, they interpreted this as showing that they could get 32 packets of crisps for their £5 (see Figure 5.2). In this case, their faulty procedure was hard to spot, as it generated an answer that was extremely close to the correct answer of 31.

To add to the confusion, children sometimes said or wrote that they had carried out a division that was different from the one they had actually carried out. Ceri and Marilyn, for example, obtained their answer of 26 bottles for the second problem as result of dividing 78 by 3. However, they later wrote that they had 'got 78p and dived [sic] it to £3.00' (see Figure 5.2).

Ceri and Marilyn also obtained the same answer, '26', for the third problem, when the correct answer was in fact four packets of biscuits. This time it was far from clear how they had obtained their answer. In order to

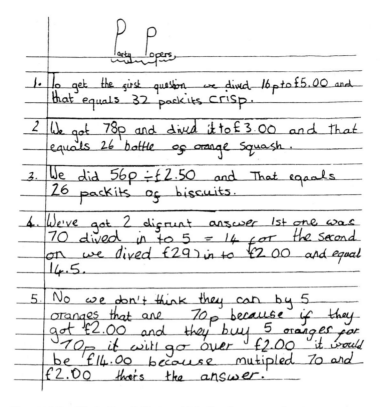

P_{arty} $P_{opers,}$

1. To get the first question we divd 16p to £5.00 and that equals 32 packits crisp.

2. We got 78p and divd it to £3.00 and that equals 26 bottle of orange squash.

3. We did 56p ÷ £2.50 and That eqaals 26 packits of biscuits.

4. We've got 2 disrunt answer 1st one was 70 dived in to 5 = 14 for the second on we dived £29? in to £2.00 and equal 14.5.

5. No we don't think they can by 5 oranges that are 70p because if they got £2.00 and they buy 5 oranges for 70p it will go over £2.00 it would be £14.00 because mutipled 70 and £2.00 thar's the answer.

Figure 5.2   'Party time!' Ceri and Marilyn's answer sheet

clarify things, the researcher who was observing the lesson asked them to show him what they had done. Marilyn explained that they had 'divided 56 into £2.50'. She was asked to do this again on the calculator. This time Marilyn entered 56 ÷ 2.50 and obtained the answer 22.4. She decided that this meant '224', and rejected this answer on the grounds that '£2.50 is not the sort of money that you could buy 224 packets of biscuits with'. She decided that her original answer of 26 was therefore correct.

In this example, Ceri and Marilyn simply ignored the decimal point on the calculator display, interpreting 22.4 as 224. Other children, however, were more perplexed when they obtained a decimal point, as they expected the division to generate a whole number for the answer. Nathan, Adam and Daniel, for example, correctly carried out the calculation 500 ÷ 16 for the first problem, but were puzzled when they obtained the answer 31.25. They suspected this meant the answer was 31 packets of crisps, and decided to check this by multiplying 31 by the price of each packet (16p). When they obtained the answer of £4.96 they were puzzled again, as they had expected it to be £5.00. After some discussion with the teacher, they realized that they were 'allowed to have change', and their understanding became somewhat clearer. As Daniel explained,

> Well, first of all we kept getting wrong answers. We, yeah, for instance we had a decimal point here which we didn't want, so we tried to work out in money how much it would cost and we couldn't get exactly £5. But we found out that we could have change, yeah, . . . so we did 31 times 16p which equals £4.96, and then we got, found out the answer was 31, 31 yeah packets.

Afterward, Heather reflected on how the lesson had gone. She said she had been surprised by how few children had successfully applied their knowledge of division.

> I would say that probably a quarter to a third attempted it successfully, and there were others who did eventually solve the problems but not in the way in which I had hoped, by dividing. A lot of them estimated, and I am not saying there is anything wrong with estimating, but in this case I was hoping that they would say 'Ah, this is like the work we did the other day, when we had all those dividing sums to do, we just divide that, that and that and there we are', and that they would make sense of the answers.

Heather had expected the children to interpret the problem as requiring division simply because they had recently been doing division in the classroom. As she said, 'I expected them to realize straight away that what we had been doing recently was linked in with this, and that it must be dividing because that's what we've been doing lately. If for no other reason!'

'Party time!': a commentary

In the 'Party time' activity, Heather presented her class with a set of word problems involving money. In the Numeracy Framework, such problems are recommended throughout Key Stage 2. In this case, Heather intended the activity to provide opportunities for children to apply their understanding of division. Heather's approach thus had some similarity with those adopted by Alice and Fiona in Chapter 4, in that all three teachers hoped the children would use a particular numerical operation in the course of the activity.

Unlike Alice and Fiona, however, Heather did not consider that 'Party time!' had been a success. Only a minority of children used the division strategy that she had intended, and many of these experienced considerable difficulty. Instead, the children often used strategies that might be seen as quite acceptable if used in real-life situations outside the classroom, such as estimating and repeated multiplication. In other words, the children may have been more successful in applying their mathematical knowledge than Heather gave them credit for.

Heather's theory of application seemed to have two main, and possibly contrasting, elements. On the one hand, she wanted to use what she termed an 'authentic' activity, on the grounds that the 'real-life' nature of the activity would facilitate the children's application. On the other hand, she assumed that the children would use division simply because they had been doing it recently – they would make a direct association with their recent work. Heather did not see herself as having an explicit role to play in this process, and she made no attempt to suggest possible strategies or intervene once the children had started.

In terms of process skills, the 'Party time' activity provides plenty of opportunities for children to make decisions about the approach to be adopted for each problem, and to check the reasonableness of their answers. Getting the children to work in small groups had also led to some interesting discussions. The activity could usefully have been extended, however, to include a plenary session in which the children talked about the methods they had used and compared the advantages and disadvantages of different approaches. Such a discussion might have helped to elicit and clarify some of the misunderstandings the children had about division. Heather herself was sensitive to such a possibility, and after the lesson suggested a possible extension activity.

> One thing I might try is perhaps to get them in their groups to explain to the rest of us what they have been doing, and perhaps if we all had calculators, and do as they tell us, and see whether they are really explaining what they want us to do. Are we really dividing 5 by 16 or 16 by 5? And so perhaps they might pick up on each other's terminology . . . I'll try to get them to listen to each other and find out what they mean.

Kathy and the VAT problem

In this example we return to Kathy, who provided us with two case studies in Chapter 3. It will be recalled that Kathy's example of a successful application was the shelving problem, in which two boys in her Year 5 class calculated the amount of shelving needed to store some science resources. Kathy used their calculations to draw up an order for the shelving, which totalled £478.17. However, she had not realized that she needed to add value added tax (VAT) (a sales tax of 17.5 per cent) to the order. She therefore decided to ask a group of three children, which included the original two boys, to work out what the VAT would be on this total. In order to do this, the children would have to apply their existing knowledge of percentages to a new situation.

In her notes before the lesson, Kathy wrote that she was 'aiming to provide an authentic activity'. As we saw in Chapter 3, Kathy considered that authentic activities were those where the children needed to know the answer for a reason. In this case, the headteacher wanted to know how much VAT to add to the order so that he would know the full cost of what he was ordering.

Kathy also wrote that she expected the children to find the activity motivating, as it was the 'follow-on to a previous authentic problem in which the children demonstrated commitment and satisfaction'. She added that she would explicitly link this activity to the previous one, in order to 'encourage engagement through connection with an activity in which they had been motivated and achieved success, with the knowledge that their work mattered and their results had been trusted by adults'. She said that her own role would be to remain approachable while monitoring the children from a distance. Once they had worked out a 'best estimate', she would 'challenge the children to convince me that they have a good estimate. I shall be trying to find ways to enable the children to reason effectively, while refusing to give my views about the correctness of the answer.' At the end, she would suggest the children check their estimate with a calculator.

During the lesson, Kathy presented the problem to the three boys, Matthew, Tim and Ali. She reminded them of their previous work in calculating the amount of shelving needed, and showed them the official order form. She explained that the school secretary had been away all week and that they needed to work out how much VAT to add to the order. She checked that they understood what VAT was, and that she wanted 'a really good estimate, the best you could possibly reach', to find out 17.5 per cent of £478.17. She told them they could use any materials they wanted, but ruled out the use of the calculator. Then she left the children to work on the problem by themselves.

The boys worked on the problem together and quickly came up with an excellent strategy. They broke down the figure of £478 into the more manageable components of 200 + 200 + 50 + 28. They started to work out 17.5 per cent of each of these components. They worked out that 17.5 per cent of 200 would be 35, and therefore 17.5 per cent of 400 would be 70. They calculated that 17.5 per cent of 50 would be 'half of 17 and a half, about 8 and three quarters', but that they still needed to take account of the remaining 28. They ended up with Tim saying, 'about 80 . . . about 83 . . . something like that . . . roughly . . . in between 82 and 85 . . . and that's our best estimate . . .'. This was in fact remarkably accurate, as the correct answer was £83.68p.

Kathy returned and asked how they were getting on.

Kathy: Right. How are we doing?
Tim: Between 82 and 85 . . . we thought that 17½ was 35, and double that again would come to 400.
Kathy: Double 35 again and that would come to 400?

> *Tim:*   No, that would come to 70, 35 doubled and that would make
>   400.
> *Kathy:* I'm not quite sure. Now I'm going to be really difficult now, I
>   don't understand anything. You need to convince me.

Kathy did not understand how the boys had arrived at their answer and
was not convinced by their estimate. She told them that the headteacher
and school secretary would also need convincing that the estimate had
been worked out carefully. She added that she understood things better
when they were written down, and that they would have to write out what
they had done. She left them with the comment, 'I need to see it visually,
not just words.'

The boys tried to write down what they had done, but found this
extremely difficult. There seemed to be some confusion as to whether they
were dealing with 'pounds' or 'percentages'. Kathy returned and worked
with them, trying to understand what they had done. However, the session was now getting somewhat lengthy, and two of the boys (Matthew
and Ali) were losing concentration. Tim finally managed to convince
Kathy that their estimate was reasonable. She allowed Matthew to check
it on the calculator, and she congratulated them on getting so close. The
lesson ended with Matthew commenting, 'Its easier to talk it and chat and
difficult to write it down.'

Afterwards, Kathy felt the lesson had gone well. She was surprised how
quickly the boys had reached their estimate, but explained that this had
only been part of her objective in the activity. 'I wanted them to convince
me that their estimate was good. I feel it is so good for children to actually
have to verbalize and prove to me and to themselves . . . to consolidate
their own thinking.'

Kathy and the VAT problem: a commentary

This example developed naturally from the case study that Kathy had provided earlier. As in the case study, she took advantage of a situation that
occurred in the everyday life of the school and turned it into a 'real-life'
problem involving money. Such problems, as we have already seen, are an
important component of the 'solving problems' strand within the Numeracy Framework. In this example, Kathy wanted the children to estimate
the VAT on the amount they had previously calculated for the shelving,
and then to explain to her how they had done this. In this she was only
partly successful. The children rapidly used their mental calculation skills
to produce a good estimate, but were unable to explain to Kathy, either by
talking or by writing, what they had done.

Kathy's theory of application remained consistent over the two examples. As before, she put great store on what she termed 'authentic activities', believing that children carrying out such activities would thereby be

motivated to apply their existing knowledge. At the same time, she did not suggest any specific strategies that the children might use, and she allowed the children to work on the problem by themselves. However, she did rule out the use of the calculator for making the estimate, a constraint that might well be interpreted as reducing the 'authenticity' of the task. In real life, the calculator is likely to be the tool which most people use when they have to calculate VAT.

In terms of developing process skills, the activity had mixed results. In the first part, the children successfully applied their existing numerical knowledge to the problem. They used an excellent strategy based on breaking down '478' into more manageable components. However, when asked to explain their reasoning, the boys were unable to communicate to Kathy what they had done, either in words or in writing. Despite Kathy's good intentions, there was little sign of the children's reasoning and communication skills being developed by this activity. In this respect, situating the activity within an 'authentic' setting was not sufficient by itself to overcome the children's difficulties.

Irene, the school field and the PE shed

Irene and her colleague Janice, who was also in the project, both taught Year 5 classes, and they worked closely together in an open-plan arrangement. During the course of the project, Irene carried out a series of activities around the topics of measurement and area. For example, she asked the children to produce a scale drawing of the school playground. She also drew on Kathy's example and asked the children to design some shelving for the classroom.

Towards the end of the project, Irene presented her children with two further problems based on features of the school. The first problem involved working out how much fertilizer would be needed to treat the school playing field. The second problem involved calculating how much paint would be needed to paint the PE shed. Both these activities involved the application of the children's knowledge about measurement and area to new situations.

In her pre-lesson questionnaire, Irene wrote that she wanted the children to 'think through' how they would go about solving the problem before they actually started work on it. This process of 'thinking through' would be elicited by way of a dialogue between each child and their teacher, in which the children would be encouraged to talk about how they would approach the problem. Irene considered that this dialogue would 'provoke the children to think through problems and order their thoughts. This will provide a structure for the application/transfer of knowledge from one idea to the next.'

In order to put this into practice, Irene worked closely with her colleague Janice. First, Irene and Janice modelled the kind of dialogue they had in mind. They carried out a short role-play, in which one acted as the 'teacher' while the other acted as the 'pupil'. In the course of this role-play, the 'teacher' elicited from the 'pupil' how she would approach an application problem that was different from the ones which the children would be working on later.

After the role-play, Irene and Janice saw each child individually and presented them with a written version of one of the two problems. Irene's problem was:

> The school field needs to have some fertilizer put on it and it needs to be spread at a rate of 10 grams for every square metre. How would you work out how much fertilizer to buy?

Janice's problem was:

> The PE shed needs to be painted. How would you work out how much paint to buy if one tin of paint covers 10 square metres?

The children generally found the school field problem easier than the PE shed problem. This was no doubt because the field was a simple two-dimensional rectangle. The shed, however, was a more complex structure, involving three dimensions and a roof with an apex (see Figure 5.3). The problems also differed in that the area of the field needed to be multiplied by ten to obtain the amount of fertilizer, while the area of the shed needed to be divided by ten to obtain the number of cans of paint.

The children approached the problems in different ways. Some children were able to consider what they needed to do in general terms, without thinking about specific quantities. For example, Gita's response to the field problem was as follows:

Gita: To work out how much fertilizer you'd need to buy you need to work out how many square metres there are in the field.

Irene: And how might you do that?

Gita: You'd measure, you might be able to work out by measuring the length of the field, the width of the field, and times them by each other, till you get the area of it.

Irene: How might you measure ?

Gita: You might measure it with a trundle wheel, or a tape measure? (There is some intervening discussion about units and measuring techniques.)

Irene: So now what?

Gita: You'd need to work out how many square metres there were on the field, to work out how many grams you'd need.

Irene: You need to tell me a little bit more . . . What sum do you need to do to work out how many grams you need?

Gita: You'd need to times the number of square metres you had by 10 grams, by ten.

Irene: All right, what would that give you?

Gita: It would give you the answer of how many grams you needed for the fertilizer for the field.

Figure 5.3   PE shed at Irene and Janice's school

Another child, Brett, approached the problems in a different way. He estimated what he thought were reasonable dimensions for the field and the shed, and then carried out the actual calculations in his head. His solution to the shed problem (see below) was an impressive piece of mental calculation. He seemed to be able to hold in his head all the different elements of the problem, and he dealt realistically with the fact that his calculations had not generated an exact number of tins of paint. However, his solution was flawed, in that he treated the shed as a regular six-sided cuboid. He failed to take into account that the roof had an apex, and that he would not be able to paint the underneath of the shed!

Brett: I'm working out in my head, like, how, just trying to make up a number of how long the shed is, and how high it is, and how wide it is. Say it was 10 metres long and 3 metres deep and 4 metres wide, then I would say, if I do the two small ends, that would be, it would be 3 times 4 on the ends, and 3 times 4 is 12, so that would be 12 square metres on each end, and that's 24 square metres. The bottom would be 4 times 10, and 4 times 10 is 40 square metres, and the sides would be 3 times 10, and that's 30, and the top would be 4 times 10, which is 40. So I've got 40 square metres on the top, and 40 on the bottom, so that's 80 square metres, and I've also got 12 and 12 on the two ends, that 24 square metres, and 24 on to 80 is 104 square metres. Then on the two sides I've got 3 times 10, and that's 30 square metres, so I've got 104 plus 60 square metres, so that's 164 square metres, and I need to work out how many tins I would need to buy, to cover the shed in paint. And I've worked out that there is 164 square metres of paint, needed to cover the shed, and there's 1 tin covers 10 square metres, and if I take away the 4 square metres and put that to the side, then I've got 160 divide by 10 make 16 tins of paint. Then I'd need one more tin of paint, so that's 17 tins of paint, and I'd be able to cover 6 more square metres with what I've got left.

Other children were less proficient in their solutions. Suzanne, for example, differed from Brett in that she tried to take account of the apex in the roof, first by removing what she termed the 'triangular bit' from her estimates, and then by adding it in again later. However, she added to her difficulties by trying to work with both centimetres and metres, and ended up with an unrealistically large quantity of paint.

Suzanne: First I would try to estimate how much paint you would need, to estimate how much wood you'd have to paint. Say the ends of the PE shed were, if you chop off the triangular bit, the end, the rectangle after, $1\frac{1}{2}$ metres, 150 centimetres by about 2 metres, and the two other sides would be about 2 metres high again, and about 3 metres lengthways, so altogether that would be, for the both sides, times the 150 by 200, and that would be . . .

Janice: You don't have to work out the answer, just say what you would do.

Suzanne: And then you'd get an answer from that, and you'd get an answer from multiply the other two sides together to get an answer and all the woodwork, including the triangle, to work out how much the triangle ends were after chopping off from the rectangle, they were about, the area about 150 square centimetres, because you would kind of add it all. And say altogether the woodwork was about 500 square centimetres, you would need 100 add, you'd have to have, five (pause) if 100 had ten pots of paint, you'd need five tens, so it would be 500 pots of paint.

Janice: Are you happy with that?

Suzanne: Yes.

Overall, Irene considered that the lesson had gone well. She was pleased that many of the children had been able to apply their understanding of area to the problems posed. She felt that most of the children had given a good account of how they might solve the problems, although their estimates of the dimensions of the field and the shed were often quite unrealistic. She also felt that the technique she and Janice had developed for eliciting the children's thinking through dialogue had worked well.

Reflecting on children such as Suzanne, who had experienced difficulty with the problems, Irene returned to her earlier ideas about providing 'structure' and helping the children 'order their thoughts'.

I think I can go back to the children and say, 'When you get a problem sit and read it, kind of order your thoughts.' And I'll have to tell them what that means you know. 'Think it through, what do you need to do first? What information is there that you don't actually need, is irrelevant for the moment? And then one step at a time.' I do, but I don't think I actually tell them to stop and think first . . . Suzanne is one you see. In her maths book she will write a lot, before we get to the reality of the situation, she's happy writing about it for a while. So we've got to try and get her to think . . . She does know, but she needs that structure still to sort it.

Irene was asked if children who needed a 'structure' in this way were actually applying their knowledge. She replied that what was important was not so much following someone else's structure, but being able to appropriate it for oneself. 'If they can only do it with a structure, they are really just going down a pathway that you could train anyone to do, just like adding up, multiplying, you're just learning. If they can make that structure for themselves and adapt it as they go along, that is application.'

The playing field and PE shed: a commentary

Irene's approach to application makes an interesting contrast with that adopted by Kathy. Like Kathy, Irene tried to use situations occurring naturally in the school as a basis for setting the children mathematical problems. However, Kathy wanted the children to solve the problem first, and then explain to her afterwards what they had done. In contrast, Irene wanted the children to explain first how they would set about solving the problem. As we have seen, Irene's approach – like Kathy's – was only partly successful.

Irene's approach to application reflects her underlying theory of application. Like Kathy, Irene felt it was important that the children were presented with 'authentic' activities. However, this was not the most central aspect of her thinking. Instead, she believed that children needed to acquire some fundamental problem-solving skills – such as identifying whether they have sufficient information – which they could apply to a problem before attempting a solution. She also felt that her role as a teacher was to help children acquire these problem-solving skills, using techniques such as modelling and posing questions. Hence she was much more interventionist in her approach than some of the other teachers in our project.

Within the Numeracy Framework, problems involving measures are an important feature of the 'solving problems' strand. The Framework provides a number of examples of 'word problems' that might be used in this respect. However, the problems used by Irene and Janice are different from most of those in the Numeracy Framework, in that they do not provide all the information needed to solve the problem. This reflects the fact that

Irene was more interested in the underlying processes than in solving the problem *per se*. In this respect, her questioning of Gita (pp. 80–1) – and particularly her use of questions such as 'How might you do that?', and 'How might you measure it?' – provides a useful model of how a teacher might suggest there are alternative ways of approaching a problem. It is also worth noting how Irene's use of phrases such as 'So now what?' and 'You need to tell me a little bit more' maintained gentle pressure on Gita to communicate her thinking. At the same time – and this might be an inevitable feature of Irene's approach – her questioning of children in isolation before they embark on a problem feels as if it might be detaching them from a more 'authentic' approach to solving the problem; for example, where they work in groups and use tools such as paper and pencil to make drawings or 'jottings' to support their thinking.

Laurie, number stories and 'Help Boxes'

Laurie taught the children in the upper half (aged 7–11 years) of a small primary school, while another teacher taught the younger pupils. In one lesson we observed, Laurie asked a group of Year 5–6 children to identify the mathematics embedded in a story that he had written for them. He then asked the children to finish the story by introducing further mathematical operations and concepts in a particular order. This activity followed on from previous work in which the class had worked on recognizing addition and subtraction in simple sentences. In his pre-lesson questionnaire, Laurie spelt out the rationale for this activity.

> I am looking at 'recognition' of maths. Part of the build-up of skills of application is to recognize the operation that needs to take place, especially where instructions are written rather than symbols. I am concerned to link mathematics to language. This is part of a whole-school project on books and stories. I hope the children will increase their knowledge of operations, and, through discussions, the links between operations.

Laurie started the lesson by reading his story to the class. It was a humorous fantasy based around one member of the class who had grown up to become a very rich farmer (see Figure 5.4). The story also contained a number of mathematical references, such as 'last year his income had tripled'. Laurie reminded the children of the work they had done earlier on recognizing mathematical operations. He said that he wanted them to read through the story he had just read, and to 'write over bits in that, when you recognize any maths'. He explained what he meant by talking them through the first mathematical operation in the story, when Robbie is trying to recall how long ago it was when he was at school with Paul. He

Looking Down the Valley

Robbie sat with his back against a tree, enjoying the morning sun as he looked over the acres that he farmed. He had just heard on his portable television that King Charles had been visited in the Palace by the new Prime Minister, Mr Paul Murray. Robbie smiled, he remembered Paul at school. How many years ago was it now? Let's see, he thought, I'm now 35 and I knew Paul when he was 10, that's 25 years ago. Paul had gone far. Mind you, so had Robbie. He was world famous now for his new breed of sheep. It was not everyone who could breed sheep with 50 per cent more wool AND a zip along its back to make it easy to get the wool off! Last year his income had tripled. If it doubled again this year (last year he had earned two million) could he afford that new farm that Annie Appleton was selling for three and a half million? . . .

Figure 5.4   Extract from Laurie's story

then divided them into groups of four, and handed out a copy of the story to each group.

After the children had completed this activity. Laurie handed out a sheet of paper to each group. On each sheet he had written a sequence of mathematical symbols. Laurie explained to the class that their task was to continue his story, but introducing mathematical ideas in the same order as the sequence he had given them. He added, 'Your story must continue with those in that sequence. Whatever else happens, that's fine, but you must use those in that order.'

There was much discussion and laughter as the children considered how they might develop the story. Laurie brought them back to order and asked if they all understood what they had to do. One boy, Callum, was worried about the triangle sign in the sequence his group had been given (see Figure 5.5). Laurie suggested that Callum think about how he might introduce a triangle into the story and reminded him of the properties of a triangle.

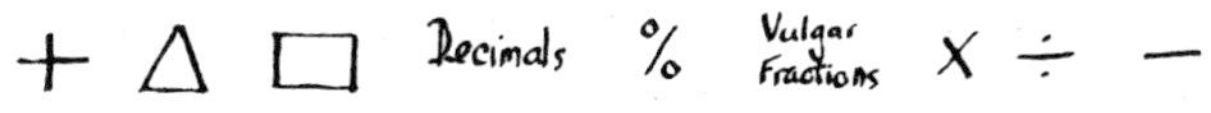

$$+ \quad \triangle \quad \square \quad \text{Decimals} \quad \% \quad \text{Vulgar Fractions} \quad \times \quad \div \quad -$$

Figure 5.5   Symbol sequence for Callum's group

The children tackled the task with some enthusiasm. Lunchtime approached and they were still working on it, so Laurie suggested they finished it after lunch. The story completed by Callum's group is shown in Figure 5.6.

"Did you know *Maths* that the job I've done for Joe who got very drunk and had a brain scan, so now he owes me five thousand pounds? *+* Add that twenty thousand that old bloke Mr.   owes me, well thats alot hey?"

"Mmmm" mused Richard, "Has that field, the *△* triangle, been sold yet?"

"No, not yet, you do mean the one with *□* 360 acres?" asked Chris "No, its not!

Decimal "So if I put a deposit on it for point five of it, thats *%* fifty percent of it which is half. I'll still be able to get it?" asked Richard

"Thats one times *x* a million" said Chris dumbly

" I'm going to share *÷* half a field with Alice and Lucy, but I'm going to subtract *−* a half of that next year!"

Figure 5.6   Completed story by Callum's group

Afterwards, Laurie said he was pleased with the way the lesson had gone. He realized that he had not allowed enough time for the activity and that more follow-up work would be needed. However, he also felt that 'some interesting stuff came out'.

Over the course of the project, Laurie continued to develop his approach to application. One of the ideas he came up with involved the children in generating and using their own 'help boxes'. Each of these boxes contained a number of cards – or 'help files' – on which the children wrote their own explanations for various mathematical operations or concepts. These included the arithmetical operations addition, subtraction, multiplication and division, as well as explanations for concepts such as averages and area (see Figure 5.7).

Laurie considered that the idea of a help box was an extension from his earlier work on 'recognizing operations'. He felt that when children were trying to solve a practical problem, they needed to be able to identify the various mathematical elements involved. The help boxes would provide

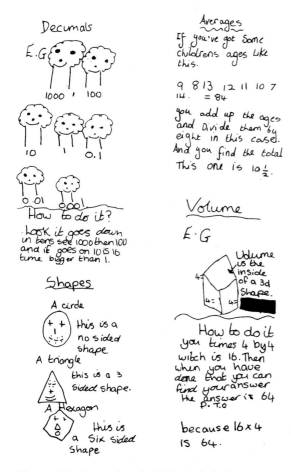

Figure 5.7 Examples of children's help files

the children with a physical reminder of what these elements might be, as well as reminding them of how to carry out the operations involved.

In the lesson we observed, the children were to use their help boxes for the first time in solving some practical problems. In the course of the lesson, Laurie wanted the children to operate at two different levels. At one level, he wanted them to solve the problems and come up with some answers. At the same time, he wanted the children to monitor their own use of their help boxes. For example, he wanted them to evaluate the usefulness of their current help files, and to identify gaps where new help files were needed. In order to assist them in this process, he had produced some evaluation sheets for monitoring the use of help boxes (see Figure 5.8).

The problems that the children were to address involved calculating the areas of different parts of a football pitch. The school was having a 'Football crazy' week, which involved a trip to their local football club and a

USING OUR MATHS HELP BOXES
NAME...
DATE...

THESE ARE THE HELP FILES THAT I USED

Area, multiplication

I MUST NOW MAKE SOME HELP FILES ON

Area of a circle,
2 squard 3 squard,
Diametar and Radars

HOW USEFUL DID YOU FIND YOUR HELP BOX

Very useful and I still am going to do some more and I looked up a lot of things.

Figure 5.8 Evaluation sheet for Annie's help box

visit from the manager of that club. The mathematics problems thus fitted with the overall theme for the week.

Laurie started the lesson by telling a gruesome story of how football had been invented. He said that long ago a man had been beheaded, and two groups of rival villagers had kicked the head from one village to the other. He explained how football pitches had evolved over the years, as more and more features were added to them, ending up with the standard design encountered today. He then handed out worksheets on which he had written various problems about the area of football pitches. Laurie also handed out the help box evaluation sheets and explained what they were for.

The children applied themselves to the problems. Some used their help boxes, but others did not. Laurie moved from group to group, intervening where he felt it appropriate. At one point he asked a group why they had not used their help boxes, and whether this was because they already knew what to do. The children chorused, 'Yes!'

Laurie stopped to talk with a group who were working on the following problem.

> If the players were spread around evenly how much space would each player have to move around in?

The group had produced an answer of 8 square yards. Laurie suggested that this was far too small, and asked how they had arrived at the answer. It turned out that the group had originally arrived at the correct answer of 366 square yards, but had rejected this as it seemed too large. Laurie found this quite interesting:

> You thought 366 was too large? But isn't it fascinating, how much space you've got in a football pitch to run in. When I watch you lot playing football I am usually screaming at you to make space, and all of you are within 10 square yards of each other, chasing the ball, and there's thousands of square yards around that you are not using. So perhaps I'll shout out that each of you has 366 square yards to move in, so use it!

Another group was trying to work out the area of the centre circle but were finding this difficult. Laurie tried to intervene:

Laurie: I told you how to work out the area of a circle, didn't I? It's πr^2. Now π is 22 over 7. Do you remember we talked about that? And r is the radius. Now let me do the radius first. What is the radius of the circle? Can you remember what radius is?

Annie: Yes, its the thing that goes from the middle to where the outside is . . . I don't know!

Laurie: It sounds like something else you could do with a card on, isn't it?

Annie: Yes.

After the lesson, the researcher talked to Annie about how she had used her help box during the activity. She explained that she had used her cards for area and multiplication when working out the area of the pitch. But she had found it harder to work out the area of the centre circle, and she had needed Laurie to explain to her about πr^2. The interview continued as follows:

> *Researcher:* Are you going to put this information about πr^2 in your box?
>
> *Annie:* Yes. It says on one of these sheets, anyone that you've forgotten to put in what could be useful and you write them down, and say, the ones you think you should write them down to remind you, so you can write them down.
>
> *Researcher:* So what are you going to put in your box about πr^2?
>
> *Annie:* Umm, I think I'll work it all out and then I'll go to Mr L (Laurie) and he'll see if it is right. Then I'll get a piece of card and you just write down what it is. And when you forget it or you need to know it, you just look through, flick them down, and you'll be able to find your πr^2 card.
>
> *Researcher:* What would the title of the card be?
>
> *Annie:* I think it might be just πr^2 . . . to find your answer when you need your answer and you don't know what it is, so you just go 'One, ummmmm, let's see, πr^2. Oh yeah! Take it out.' So you take it out!

Laurie reflected later on how the lesson had gone. He explained that the activity had not only provided the children with an opportunity to use their help boxes to solve problems, but it had provided an opportunity for them to evaluate the contents of their boxes:

> And it was a fascinating lesson because suddenly lots of children were saying, which was what I'd hoped, 'I haven't got that in my box', or 'No, I don't understand what I've written'. And I think that was really the purpose overall in what we were doing. Really a way of them assessing their own ability.

Laurie considered that Annie had used her help box well. He felt that for her, the cards had served as a physical reminder of the mathematics she was supposed to apply. He also commented on how several children had been able to 'break down' the problems they were working on, in order to recognize the different mathematical operations involved. He added, 'I think that one of the problems we get in application is that if the application has more than one mathematical tool in there, there is a lot of confusion.'

Laurie explained that his approach to the application of mathematics was closely related to one he had developed to help children with writing. He said that in writing they had used all sorts of narrative devices –

storytelling, drama and cartoon strips – as well as processes such as conferencing, drafting and redrafting. He felt that there were strong parallels with what the children were doing with their help boxes. When asked for an example of how they might use drama, Laurie described some work he had done on decimals:

> I asked my Year 6 to see if they could explain what decimals were. They decided to use the fairly standard one really, one person being 1000, another person being 100, and that person being ten times better than that person, and place value going down. And they had a whole group of them, until one was 0.1, 0.01, one was 0.01 and so on. What they tried to get across was that each person was ten times bigger or ten times smaller than the person next to them . . . but what was fascinating was that when I asked them to write their help cards, then they actually drew people of different sizes, to signify place value. They had actually taken the concept of the story and put it on their help cards' [see Figure 5.7].

Number stories and help boxes: a commentary

We have just seen two examples of the ways in which Laurie attempted to promote application. In the first lesson, Laurie asked his class to identify the mathematics in a story he had written, and to write an extension to the story incorporating specific mathematical operations and concepts in a particular sequence. This activity can thus be seen as an extension to the much simpler 'number stories' that Barbara and Diane were eliciting from their Year 1 classes (see Chapter 4). Generating 'number stories' is also a suggested activity within the 'solving problems' strand of the Numeracy Framework, although Laurie's approach appears to offer more scope for exercising children's imagination than some of the examples given in this.

In the second lesson, the children were given the opportunity to use and evaluate the help boxes that they had developed to support their application of particular mathematical operations. These help boxes provide opportunities for meeting the Numeracy Framework's objective that pupils should be able to 'explain methods and reasoning about numbers orally and in writing' (DfEE 1999, section 6: 76). Again, though, it appears that Laurie's approach is more complex and imaginative than many of the examples provided in the Numeracy Framework.

Both the lessons were underpinned by Laurie's own theories about application. He believed that a central part of being able to apply mathematics is the ability to recognize mathematics in situations, particularly when these are presented as written instructions. Both these activities were therefore aimed at developing recognition skills. Moreover, Laurie believed that the notion of 'story' was of central importance in making connections between mathematics and situations. Hence, in the first lesson, the children were not only required to recognize mathematical operations in the story he had written, but they had also to generate their own stories incorporating particular operations. This idea was developed further through the help boxes, where the children were being asked to write explanations for themselves of particular mathematical operations or concepts. These help boxes then had a physical existence independent of any particular problem; they could be carried around, flicked through, taken out, used, rejected or modified as appropriate. Underlying this approach is the idea of mathematics as a 'tool kit', and the process of application as one of selecting an appropriate 'tool' for the job in hand.

Overview

In this chapter we have presented examples of how four teachers at Key Stage 2 developed their practice in the area of application. As in Chapter 4, we have provided commentaries on these examples in terms of the nature and purposes of the activities, the teachers' theories and practice concerning application, and the opportunities for developing the process skills of decision making, communication and reasoning. We have also indicated where each activity might be situated within the objectives of the Numeracy Framework. Teachers attempting to implement this might find these examples useful starting points.

As in Chapter 4, the four teachers described in this chapter present four very contrasting approaches to application. Heather, for example, used word problems involving money in order to encourage children to apply their recently acquired knowledge of division. Kathy, in contrast, used a naturally occurring money problem within the school as an opportunity for children to make an estimate and explain their reasoning. Irene also used features of the school as a basis for setting problems for the children: however, she was more concerned with getting the children to think through their approaches to the problems than with their solutions. Finally, Laurie used both number stories and help boxes to develop children's ability to recognize and articulate mathematical operations. Clearly, as with the teachers at Key Stage 1, there was little consensus among these teachers as to how application might best be developed in the classroom.

Yet despite this lack of consensus, the issues emerging at Key Stage 2 are very similar to those that emerged at Key Stage 1. For example, Kathy's development of the shelving problem raises again the question of how far a teacher can introduce 'real life' into the classroom and how far this is desirable. Heather's use of 'Party time!' provides another example of the conflict between providing practice in one particular operation and allowing children to choose between different operations: it also raises the issue of what a teacher might do if children fail to 'apply' in the ways intended. Irene's questioning of the children raises the issues of how and when teachers should intervene to promote application. Finally, all four examples remind us in their different ways that the development of process skills – and particularly those that involve reasoning – is by no means a straightforward matter. We shall return to these issues again in Chapter 7.

6

Teaching for application in Japan

In this chapter we provide an illustration of the Japanese approach to teaching mathematics in primary schools. In particular, we examine the extent to which the application of mathematical knowledge is seen as a problem in Japan, and we look at ways in which application is approached by some Japanese teachers in their classrooms. The chapter is based on observations made during a visit to Japan by two members of the research team.

Our observations of Japanese practice are particularly relevant to current developments in primary mathematics in England and Wales. As we saw in Chapter 2, the recent concern about standards of numeracy has been fuelled by suggestions that English pupils perform poorly compared with their counterparts in countries such as Korea, Taiwan and Japan. As a result, the Numeracy Task Force proposed that the kind of teaching methods used in these countries – based around whole class teaching – should be widely adopted in England and Wales:

> Teaching the whole class does not mean that the teacher simply 'lectures' the class. Good direct teaching with the whole class is characterised by genuine communication about mathematics . . . Some of the countries that do best in international comparisons, such as Japan and Korea, report a high frequency of lessons in which children work together as a class, and respond to one another.
>
> (DfEE 1998a: 19)

One of our main reasons for visiting Japan was to observe Japanese teaching methods at first hand and draw our own conclusions about their relevance for raising standards of numeracy in England and Wales. At the same time, we wanted to explore the issue of application in the Japanese context. We wanted to know what conceptions of application are held by Japanese teachers and educators, and we wanted to see how Japanese teachers approach application in the classroom.

The Japanese education system

The Japanese education system is highly centralized, with a national curriculum that is revised every ten years or so. All teachers are required to follow this curriculum and textbooks can only be used in schools if they have been authorized by the Japanese Ministry of Education (Monbushu). However, individual teachers have a certain amount of discretion in deciding what teaching methods, materials and resources they will use in a particular lesson.

In Japan, children attend primary (or elementary) school between the ages of 6 and 12 years. Classroom practice in these schools is underpinned by two fundamental principles:

- all children are taught in same-age, mixed ability classes;
- the whole class proceeds at the same pace.

The first principle means that there is no setting or streaming according to children's ability. The second principle means that, for any given lesson, all the children in the class are being taught the same part of the curriculum. Both principles reflect the fundamental aim of Japanese state education of ensuring that all pupils have reached a minimum level of attainment by the end of compulsory schooling at 15 years of age.

Running alongside the state education system is an extensive system of private education, most notably in the form of evening classes (Juku). A large number of Japanese children attend Juku, for up to two or three hours a time on three evenings a week. As can be imagined, the egalitarian aims and practice of the state education system do not sit easily alongside a flourishing private sector available for those who are willing and able to pay for it.

Observing in Japanese classrooms

Our observations of Japanese practice are based on visits we made to six elementary schools in three different regions of Japan. During these visits, we observed 11 mathematics lessons: five at Year 1 (ages 6–7 years), four at Year 4 (ages 9–10 years) and two at Year 5 (ages 10–11 years). We also interviewed most of the teachers before and after each lesson. The interviews focused on what was planned for the lesson and how the teacher felt it had gone. At the same time, we also asked more general questions about mathematics teaching and application. The interviews were carried out through interpreters, and these interpreters also observed the lessons with us and gave a running commentary (in English) on to a tape recorder. During the lesson, we asked our interpreter questions about particular incidents, and took extensive notes and photographs. Afterwards, we used all these sources of information to construct a detailed account of what had taken place during the lesson.

As can be seen, our observations in Japanese classrooms were not directly comparable with the lessons we observed in England as part of our 'using and applying' project (see Chapters 4–5). As visitors to Japan, we were not in a position to choose the schools, the teachers or the lessons we were going to observe. In addition, while the English teachers had committed themselves to a project focusing specifically on application, the Japanese teachers had committed themselves to nothing more than being observed and interviewed on a single visit. Nevertheless, there were still sufficient commonalities in what we saw, across very different parts of the country, to suggest that we were observing some typical Japanese practice.

The lessons we observed all tended to follow a common structure, proceeding through most (if not all) of the following stages.

1 The teacher recaps previous lesson(s) and/or tests the children on what they have remembered.
2 The teacher presents the main purpose of the lesson – usually by writing something on the blackboard – and discusses this with the class.
3 The children are presented with a task (or game) that is relevant to the main purpose of the lesson.
4 The children work on their task (or play the game), individually, in pairs or in small groups.
5 The teacher calls the class together. The children describe what they have done, and present their solutions to the class. There is usually a discussion of the advantages and disadvantages of different solutions.
6 Steps 3, 4 and 5 might be repeated.
7 The teacher ends the lesson by summarizing what has been learnt.

As can be seen, this structure is quite similar to that proposed in the Numeracy Framework for the daily mathematics lesson in English primary schools. In Japan, the same structure was seen in both the Year 1 classes and the Year 4–5 classes, although there were some differences according to the age of the children. For the Year 1 classes, the teachers tended to present the children with a number of relatively short activities (a few minutes each), which all linked to the overall theme of the lesson (for example, numbers that added to 10). For the Year 4–5 classes, the teachers tended to present the children with a single activity on which they would work for most of the lesson. For both age groups, lessons lasted for around 40–45 minutes.

Most of the resources used during the lessons tended to support collaborative rather than individual working. Perhaps the most striking example of this was the extensive use made of the blackboard. These boards stretched across most of the width of the classroom, and were made of a magnetic material, enabling various magnetic objects (such as number cards) to be displayed as well as writing in chalk. The boards were used both by teachers and children during the lesson, and served as a kind of communal workspace for the whole class. In contrast, we saw relatively few instances of children working individually on workbooks or using individual workcards. We also saw no instances of children using calculators or computers.

Some of the teachers used overhead projectors (OHPs) as well as the blackboard to display pictures, diagrams or examples of the children's work. In one lesson, we observed a teacher using two OHPs side by side. She gave the children in her Year 4 class the problem of displaying some information in the form of a table. The information was provided by the school textbook, and concerned the location, type and frequency of accidents in a school. The children worked in small groups to generate tables on sheets of paper. The teacher used a photocopier to make transparencies of some of the children's solutions, and used the two OHPs to display two solutions side by side. The children discussed the solutions and agreed that one table was a better way of displaying information than the other.

Mrs Okura: numbers that add to six

The following lesson provides a good example of the Year 1 lessons that we observed. The lesson was taught by Mrs Okura, and was concerned entirely with number bonds that added to six (3 + 3, 2 + 4 and so on).

In the pre-lesson interview, Mrs Okura explained her plan for the lesson. She said that before the children were introduced to addition and subtraction, they needed a concept of number. In a previous lesson, they had worked on number bonds that made five. For today's lesson, the focus would be on six.

Mrs Okura explained that she would start by reviewing what the children knew about five. She would then introduce the basic idea of the lesson in a concrete situation, by taking two sweets from a tin containing six sweets and asking the children how many remained. She thought that some children would be able to answer at this stage, but most would not. The children would then play two different games, both of which involved numbers adding up to six. After this, they would do some exercises from their textbooks. Finally, she would 'confirm' what they had learned during the lesson. When asked what she would do with those who already possessed the necessary understanding at the start of the lesson, she replied, 'Nothing special – the aim is for the whole class.' When asked about application, she said that the games would provide a context for the children to apply what they knew.

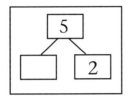

Figure 6.1   Flash card used by Mrs Okura for testing number bonds of five

When we arrived in the classroom, there were 23 children seated in rows and facing the front. Mrs Okura followed her lesson plan closely. First she tested the children's knowledge of number bonds to five by holding up large flash cards (see Figure 6.1) and asking the children to call out the missing numbers. Next, she put six sweets in a large tin, at which point the children called out, 'I want to eat!' Mrs Okura said that she wanted to eat two sweets, at which the children replied, 'It's not fair!' She asked the class how many sweets were left in the tin after she had taken two out. Some children said 'three', while one boy stood up and said 'four'. Mrs Okura showed them the inside of the can, with four sweets stuck to the bottom. She went to the board and wrote up the aim of the lesson: 'to find out what numbers make six'. She also explained, 'today's aim is to understand the combinations of six, so we know without looking in the box. We will learn through games.'

Mrs Okura then introduced the first game. The children moved their desks around so they were facing each other in pairs. Each pair had six sweets in an open box on the desk between them. Mrs Okura told them to place their hands under the table. When she said 'Go!', they were to grab as many sweets as they could. Each member of the pair then called out how many sweets they had managed to grab. This was repeated several times, to great excitement all round. Each time, Mrs Okura recorded the various combinations on the board, using yellow magnetic blocks (see Figure 6.2).

Mrs Okura placed magnetic cards with numerals on them next to each combination. The children called out that the numbers were in the wrong order, so she reorganized them to produced the arrangement shown in Figure 6.3.

Mrs Okura chalked on the blackboard to make connections between the same combinations in different orders (for example, 2 + 4 and 4 + 2). She pointed out that there was only one combination of 3 + 3. However, some of the children called out, 'There are two threes, so they have friends!' A further discussion of all the combinations ensued.

Mrs Okura then introduced the second game. The children again worked in pairs, facing each other. Each pair had a small set of cards, which they dealt out face down on the desk in front of them. Each child

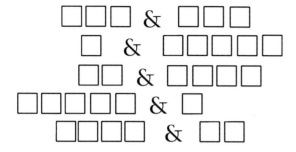

Figure 6.2   Magnetic blocks on the blackboard in Mrs Okura's lesson

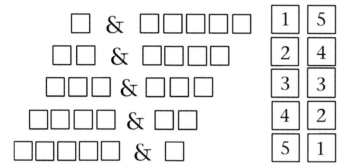

Figure 6.3   Magnetic blocks and numeral cards on the blackboard, re-ordered

took it in turns to turn over one card, then find another that when added to the first card made a total of six. The children had played this game in a previous lesson, looking for numbers that added to five, and several of them continued to look for combinations of five rather than six. This was somewhat surprising, given the clear focus of the lesson on six, and Mrs Okura had to explain the game more carefully for these children.

For the next part of the lesson, the children turned their desks back to face the front again. Mrs Okura asked them to open their textbooks at page 23 and complete some examples there. All the examples required the children to fill in numbers that added to six. Mrs Okura moved around the class, correcting their work where necessary.

In the final stage of the lesson, Mrs Okura reviewed what had been learnt. She asked the children what they had found out about the combinations. One child went to the front and pointed to the number combinations on the board, saying:

Child: The order of the numbers is completely in reverse. One to five on the left and five to one on the right. And the sum of these numbers is six.

Mrs Okura: It means that the left-hand side increases and the right-hand side decreases ... If one person takes a lot of candies, the other cannot.

Mrs Okura tested the children using large flash cards similar to those used at the start of the lesson but with combinations of six rather than five. She first asked the whole class to call out the missing numbers, and then asked individual children. One boy had worked very well, so he was rewarded by being allowed to wear a small imitation 'mortarboard' which Mrs Okura produced from the corner of the classroom. The boy called out, 'I am proud', and his classmates applauded. Mrs Okura finished the lesson by telling the children, 'If you know the combination of these numbers, it will help you in real life.'

Afterwards, we asked Mrs Okura if the lesson had achieved its aims. She said she was not sure it had achieved all she had hoped for, in that some of the children still did not seem to know all the combinations of six. But she felt they had at least learned that two numbers added up to six, and that there was a rule underlying this. She said she would provide more opportunities for children to practise these combinations before moving on to other numbers.

As can be seen, Mrs Okura's lesson followed closely the structure described earlier (see p. 96). She started the lesson by recapping on what had been learned in the previous lesson, and then explained the purpose of the current lesson to the class. She used a number of different activities to achieve this purpose, and she used the information generated by the children when playing the games as an integral part of the lesson. Finally, she reviewed what the children had learned during the lesson.

Mrs Okura's lesson was typical of the other Year 1 lessons that we observed in that it focused entirely on a single piece of mathematics: number bonds to six. Indeed, we were struck by the similarity of the Year 1 lessons in different parts of Japan. We saw two lessons that focused on number bonds to 10, and another lesson that focused on number bonds to 7. In each case, the Year 1 teachers followed a similar approach to that of Mrs Okura, using a range of games and whole class activities to achieve their aims.

There was one Year 1 teacher, however, who adopted a somewhat different approach. This teacher, Mrs Ashino, wanted to use concrete examples to introduce the children to the formal notation of arithmetic, and specifically to the signs for + and = . She used the OHP and started by displaying a picture of five fish in a tank; three on one side and two on the other. She asked the children to produce a story about the fish, but was a bit dismayed when they produced non-mathematical stories such as, 'They look beautiful in the water.' She modelled the story she had been looking for. 'Three fish came and another two came. How many fish are there altogether?' Mrs Ashino then wrote on the board:

$$3 + 2 = 5$$

and asked the children to chant this after her. She used magnetic blocks to demonstrate this addition on the board, and asked the children to copy her using their own sets of blocks. She then got them to write the sum in their workbooks. This whole cycle was repeated twice more, with Mrs Ashino first showing pictures on the OHP (one child joining three more on a long sofa, two plates containing five apples and four apples) and then writing on the board how these additions could be represented. Finally, Mrs Ashino ended the lesson by handing out some worksheets (copied from the textbook) containing addition sums for the children to complete.

Mr Takamatsu: a formula for ratio

The second lesson that we describe in detail was taught by Mr Takamatsu and concerned the topic of ratio. It is in many ways typical of the Year 4–5 lessons that we observed.

Before the lesson, Mr Takamatsu produced a lesson plan that he had written out for us in English. The plan explained that the session was concerned with 'the general idea of ratio', and that he would present two 'real-life' problems to the pupils. Each of these problems could be solved using the formula $A (1 \pm B/C)$.

The first problem involved ribbons. Each child would be given two ribbons of length 24 cm, and asked to calculate the length of 1 ribbon and $3/4$ of a ribbon. Mr Takamatsu said he would use their solutions to introduce the formula shown above. The second problem involved money. The children would be told that a student took 4000 yen on a school excursion and spent $3/5$ of it on the first day. How much did she have left? Again, the formula would be introduced as a way of solving the problem. Mr Takamatsu thought that all the children would be able to understand the formula by the end of the lesson.

The class consisted of 28 children, who were seated in a horseshoe arrangement around the teacher's desk. Mr Takamatsu gave the children two ribbons each and wrote the problem in Japanese on the board:

> You have two ribbons and each of them is 24 centimetres long. Now you cut $3/4$ off one ribbon and attach it to the other ribbon. What is the length of the long ribbon you have just made?

Mr Takamatsu also fixed two strips of card, of equal length, on to the board using magnetic discs. He divided one of the strips into quarters, as shown in Figure 6.4. These strips were intended to help the children think about the ribbon problem.

After discussing the problem with the class, Mr Takamatsu asked them

Figure 6.4 Two strips of card used in Mr Takamatsu's lesson

to work on it themselves. The children worked in groups of two or three, discussing the problem together. The class felt motivated and busy. After 10 minutes or so, Mr Takamatsu asked a boy to demonstrate his solution on the board. He wrote:

$$24 \div 4 = 6$$
$$6 \times 3 = 18$$
$$24 + 18 = 42$$

Mr Takamatsu asked whether other pupils had used this method. Several raised their hands. Mr Takamatsu asked two pupils – who had *not* raised their hands – to come to the board and explain this method, which they did. He then asked another boy to demonstrate his method. The boy wrote:

$$24 \div 4 = 6$$
$$6 \times 7 = 42$$

As before, Mr Takamatsu asked other pupils to explain this boy's method. One pupil did so by going to the board and dividing up the strip on the left-hand side into four quarters (see Figure 6.5). He then counted seven quarters to indicate the total length of the joined ribbons. The other pupils clapped at this point, indicating their agreement and understanding of his solution.

Figure 6.5 Two strips of card, both marked in quarters

A girl stepped forward and wrote up her solution as

$$24 \times {}^3/_4 + 24 = 42$$

Mr Takamatsu asked other pupils to explain this. A boy went to the front and said that there were 'two 24s', indicating with his hands the connection between the parts of the girl's solution and the strips of card on the board. Mr Takamatsu made the connections more explicit by drawing a chalk line between the second 24 of the formula and the left-hand ribbon.

Two more pupils presented their solutions. Both were different from the ones already described. Each time Mr Takamatsu asked other pupils if they understood, and to explain the solutions to the rest of the class.

Finally, one girl spontaneously produced the solution that Mr Takamatsu was particularly interested in. She went to the board and wrote:

$$24 \times 1^3/_4 = 24 \times {}^7/_4 = {}^{42}/_1 = 42$$

Mr Takamatsu asked those who understood this solution to stand up. Several pupils did so. He then asked those who were still sitting down to ask for explanations from those who were standing up. Various conversations took place between the pupils. Mr Takamatsu returned to the girl who had produced this solution and asked for her explanation. She explicitly connected the $1^3/_4$ in her solution to the two strips on the board. Mr Takamatsu reinforced this by drawing a chalk line between her $1^3/_4$ and the two strips. Finally, he wrote the formula $24 (1 + {}^3/_4)$ on the board and asked the children to copy this down in their books.

The lesson was nearly over, but Mr Takamatsu still introduced his second problem, concerning the girl on the school excursion. He told the class they would continue working on this problem in the next lesson, and that he wanted them to solve it by using just one formula.

Afterwards, Mr Takamatsu explained that the lesson had only partially met his aims. He had expected more children to come up with the formula $(1 + {}^3/_4)$ earlier in the lesson. He said he would continue this approach in the next lesson, focusing on the 'minus' in the formula rather than the 'plus'.

Mr Takamatsu also said that the methods he had used in the lesson were 'typical of Japanese lessons'. When asked about his technique of getting children to explain each other's methods, he said, 'Expressing other people's ideas is the perfect way to understand something. Listening doesn't make for good understanding. Children go to the board and explain, and there is no shame about getting it wrong, no embarrassment . . . We don't laugh at an opinion.'

As with Year 1, there were strong similarities between this lesson and those of the other Year 4–5 teachers. Another Year 5 teacher also used lengths of ribbon in his lesson, although he had a different focus. He was introducing his class to the idea of multiplying by decimals, and posed them the problem, 'If 1 metre of ribbon costs 80 yen, what does 1.2 metres cost?' A similar problem was used by a Year 4 teacher, although in her case it involved bottles of Coca-Cola: 'If 1 litre of Coca-Cola costs 200 yen, how much does 1.5 litres cost?' Both these teachers followed a similar approach to Mr Takamatsu, in that the children first attempted the problems on their own or in small groups. Next, they took turns to come to the board and demonstrate their solutions. Finally, the teachers discussed how some ways of attempting the problem were more useful than others.

How is application perceived in Japan?

We tried in our interviews to elicit the Japanese teachers' perceptions of application. This proved to be unexpectedly difficult, mainly because it seemed that the concept of 'application' was not one with which the teachers were very familiar. In this respect, they may have been influenced by the curriculum they were teaching: we were subsequently informed that the idea of 'application' does not feature in the Japanese national curriculum for primary mathematics.

We attempted to convey our meaning of the term by talking about children applying what they learned in school to everyday life outside school. Most of the teachers replied that this was not a major problem in Japan. One teacher of Year 1 said that children did not have any problems using mathematics outside school. For example, young children were taught by their parents how to use money when they were out shopping. Another Year 1 teacher apologized for not teaching a lesson about application, adding that it was not relevant for children at this age. A Year 4 teacher said that application was not usually a problem, particularly for areas such as money. However, she admitted that there was sometimes a problem teaching decimals to her children, as they did not use them in real life.

When asked what, if anything, they did to help children with application, the teachers gave two main kinds of response. Some pointed out that they always tried to introduce a new mathematical concept in a practical or 'real-life' setting, as in the Year 4–5 lesson described above. However, the rationale for this approach seemed to be primarily in terms of helping the children understand the concept, rather than as a means of teaching for application of the concept. The other main kind of response was to talk in terms of making links between mathematics and other areas of the curriculum, such as science and 'home-making'. For example, the headteacher of one school explained that the mathematics and science curricula in his school were very close, so that when pupils learned in mathematics about graphs, for example, they could use this knowledge in science.

Mr Takamatsu, whose lesson we described above, appeared to take application more seriously than the other teachers. When asked whether application was a problem in Japan he replied, 'It's kind of a problem. It's important to apply.' He described how he introduced new concepts in practical contexts. For example, he would introduce the concept of averages by measuring and comparing the pupils' steps, and he would introduce ideas about area by measuring the school playground. In addition, he showed us a booklet he had produced for the children with examples of how the mathematics learned in school might be applied outside school. He gave the example of volume, and said he wanted his pupils to have a 'feeling for volume – so they know how much water is in a bath or a pool'.

A somewhat broader perspective on the problem of application emerged from our interviews with two professors of mathematics education. Both professors thought that the application of mathematics was indeed a problem in Japan, but that it did not necessarily show itself in the elementary school. For example, when asked if application was a problem in Japan, one professor replied:

> Yes. The same thing is true in Japan as in England. For 10-year-olds, maths is necessary for everyday life, and there is no problem at that level. But for older students in lower secondary school, it is difficult ... [many pupils] do not like maths, do not understand maths, and do not understand why they have to study maths.

A similar point was made by the other professor. He said that application was a problem in Japan, and that too much emphasis was placed on calculation at the expense of application: 'One problem is that many children do not like maths. I think, because teachers emphasise calculation. After Grade 6 the content becomes very abstract, so children dislike the content of maths.'

Both professors agreed that Japanese teachers could do more to make connections between the mathematics they were teaching and the ways in which this mathematics might be used in everyday life or in other areas of the curriculum. At the same time, they recognized that this was difficult to do, and that many teachers did not give this priority.

Overview

In this chapter we have looked at the way in which mathematics is taught in Japanese elementary schools. Our observations make clear that lessons typically follow a structure similar to that advocated within the Numeracy Framework in England and Wales. Key features of the Japanese approach include a clear and explicit focus to the lesson, the use of resources that support collaborative rather than individual learning, and high levels of teacher–pupil and pupil–pupil interaction. Moreover, our observations suggest that this approach was well received by the pupils (who were for the most part on-task, attentive and well motivated) and that it was carried out by the teachers with enthusiasm, efficiency and good humour. At the same time, we had some concerns that high-achieving pupils were not always being stretched, and that low-achieving pupils were not necessarily understanding all that was going on.

Two important questions are raised by these Japanese teaching methods. Do they explain the relatively high performance of Japanese pupils in international surveys? And will they raise standards of numeracy if they are introduced in England and Wales? Our observations do not allow us to provide definitive answers to these questions. Nevertheless, our visit to Japan suggested there may be a wide range of factors – in addition to teaching methods – that might contribute to the country's high performance in international surveys. These factors include the high value placed on education within Japanese society, the nature of the curriculum, the widespread attendance at Juku and the high status that teachers are afforded in Japan. Moreover, it is clear that Japanese teaching methods have developed to fit the particular conditions of Japanese state education. For example, given that there is an underlying principle that the whole class proceeds through the curriculum at the same speed, it follows that whole class teaching approaches will be employed. We have therefore no reason to suppose that teaching methods that have evolved to suit the needs of Japan will transplant in a straightforward and unproblematic way to the education system of England and Wales.

With respect to application, our observations and interviews provide a somewhat puzzling picture. On the one hand, the Japanese teachers did not seem to think that application was a problem, thus reflecting the lack of explicit attention given to it within the Japanese curriculum. In addition, their main conceptualizations of 'teaching for application' seemed to be limited to introducing new concepts by means of concrete examples and making links across the curriculum. On the other hand, a closer inspection of their practice suggests that it did indeed provide opportunities for children to apply their mathematical knowledge to a range of practical problems. In addition, the techniques demonstrated by teachers such as Mr Takamatsu placed great emphasis on children explaining their thinking – as well as the thinking of other children – in a highly interactive setting. Nevertheless, the fact that two leading Japanese mathematics educators believe there is a problem of application in Japan suggests that Japanese methods do not by themselves constitute a complete solution to the problem of application.

Application in theory and practice

In this book we have looked at the problem of application in mathematics from a number of different perspectives. We have seen how application is conceptualized within different theories of learning, and the way in which it has been treated within the mathematics curriculum in England and Wales. We have described in some detail the approaches taken to application by a group of English primary school teachers as they tried to develop their practice in this area. As a contrast, we have also looked at the way in which application is viewed by teachers and educators in Japan.

In this chapter we bring these different perspectives together, seeking areas of overlap and agreement as well as noting areas of conflict and disagreement. We start by looking at the different ways in which application has been conceptualized within theories of learning and within the mathematics curriculum. Next, we compare these conceptualizations with the approaches to application adopted by the English teachers in our project and by teachers in Japan. Finally, we turn to the practical implications of this work, and look at some of the issues and dilemmas involved in teaching for application in the classroom.

How is application conceptualized?

At the start of the book we defined the problem of application in the following way: *people frequently have difficulty applying mathematical knowledge acquired in one context to problems posed in another.* In Chapter 1 we presented evidence from a range of research studies that illustrated these difficulties. We also showed that such difficulties are not just restricted to mathematics, but can be found across a number of different domains of knowledge.

In the course of this book we have seen many more examples of both successful and unsuccessful application. Such examples are not hard to find. As we saw in Chapter 3, the teachers in our project had little difficulty in locating in their daily practice instances of children who were successfully applying their mathematical knowledge, as well as children who were not. Even in our brief visit to Japan, we saw examples of successful and unsuccessful application. Indeed, one of the most striking episodes of the visit occurred when some children in Mrs Okura's Year 1 class started to play a game by looking for numbers that added to five, as they had in a previous lesson, rather than numbers adding to six, which was the focus of the current lesson (see p. 99). The children had 'transferred' their knowledge of the game from one lesson to another, but had not adapted this knowledge appropriately to meet the requirements of the new activity.

How is the problem of application conceptualized within theories of learning? In Chapter 1 we looked at application from three contrasting theoretical perspectives: those of associationism, constructivism and situated cognition. From the associationist perspective, as we saw, learning is regarded as a process of making links, or connections, between small elements of experience. From this point of view, the successful transfer of knowledge to a new situation depends on the amount of similarity between elements of the new situation and associations that have already been acquired. From the associationist perspective, transfer to very different situations is unlikely to occur. In contrast, from the constructivist perspective learning is regarded as a process whereby learners construct from experience increasingly powerful and more general intellectual structures. Once acquired, these intellectual structures can then be applied to a range of situations, even if these are very different from those already encountered. From the constructivist point of view, transfer to new situations should not be too problematic. The third theoretical perspective, situated cognition, differs from both associationism and constructivism in arguing that knowledge is essentially situated in the social contexts in which it is acquired or used. From this perspective, the notion that knowledge can be 'transferred' from one situation to another is incoherent, resting as it does on a faulty assumption about the nature of knowledge. Instead, the situated cognition perspective suggests that teachers should aim to introduce learners to the 'authentic working practices' of particular cultures; in this case, mathematics as it is practised by mathematicians.

As can be seen, there is no obvious consensus between these different perspectives. Each theory makes different predictions about the amount of transfer that might be expected. Each theory also makes different recommendations about what teachers might do. These theories of learning provide interesting perspectives on the problem of application, but they do not provide definitive answers.

How has application been conceptualized within the mathematics curriculum in England and Wales? As we saw in Chapter 2, successive versions of the National Curriculum have attempted to address this issue through a separate strand entitled 'Using and Applying Mathematics'. This strand attempted to ensure that all pupils had opportunities to 'use and apply mathematics in practical tasks, in real-life problems and within mathematics itself' (DfE 1995: 2). Particular emphasis was placed on the process skills of decision making, communication about mathematics, and reasoning. In contrast, the Numeracy Framework, introduced into primary schools as part of the National Numeracy Strategy, has taken a different approach to application. 'Using and Applying Mathematics' is no longer a separate strand, although many of the elements of 'using and applying' can still be found under the 'solving problems' strand of the Numeracy Framework.

To what extent are these approaches to application within the curriculum underpinned by a particular theoretical perspective on learning? As we saw in Chapter 2, it is hard to find explicit evidence of any theoretical perspective underpinning either the National Curriculum or the National Numeracy Strategy. We did suggest, however, that the emphasis on processes within 'Using and Applying Mathematics' has some resonance with ideas derived from the perspective of situated cognition. We also suggested that the approach underlying the Numeracy Framework was more akin to that of associationism. The overriding impression that remains, however, is that the designers of the Numeracy Framework do not consider that application in mathematics is in any sense problematic. Instead, it seems to be assumed that if pupils are taught according to the ways laid down in the Numeracy Framework, then they will experience little difficulty in applying their knowledge in later life. And yet all the research evidence on application suggests that this is a dangerous assumption.

The teachers' approaches to application

In Chapters 3, 4 and 5 we looked at the ways in which a group of experienced and well motivated teachers developed their practice in the area of application. What can we now say about the approaches adopted by these teachers? And how do their approaches to teaching for application relate to the conceptualizations of application found in curriculum documents and theories of learning?

As we saw earlier, there was a great diversity in the approaches adopted by the project teachers. There was clearly no consensus in the group as to the 'right' way to approach application, nor did we attempt to impose one. At the same time, we can still identify some shared ideas and recurring themes amid this diversity.

The project teachers placed considerable importance on the *activities* that they designed to promote application in the classroom. These activities included games, problems involving money and measures, real-life simulations, investigations and writing number stories. The teachers worked hard at planning these activities, and often spent a considerable amount of time constructing the necessary materials. They also put a lot of ingenuity and originality into this work. They were not simply carrying out a standard lesson taken from a curriculum document or commercial mathematics scheme.

What purpose were these activities intended to serve? For the most part, the teachers saw them as providing *opportunities for children to apply existing mathematical knowledge in a new context*. Some teachers wanted the children to use a particular mathematical concept or operation that the children had recently been working on in the classroom, and they therefore devised an activity that required the use of this concept or operation. For example, Alice wanted her children to apply their knowledge of subtraction in the car boot sale (Chapter 4, pp. 52–6), while Heather wanted her children to use their knowledge of division in the 'Party time!' activity (Chapter 5, pp. 72–6). Other teachers were more open-ended in their approaches, allowing – and in some cases encouraging – the children to choose between different concepts or operations. For example, this open-endedness could be found in Claire's wine gums investigation (Chapter 3, pp. 39–41) or in Kathy's shelving and VAT problems (Chapter 3, pp. 43–4 and Chapter 5, pp. 76–9).

There were some occasions, however, where the teachers adopted a rather different approach. Here, their main concern was *to help children organize and reflect on their existing mathematical knowledge*. In other words, they were trying to help children acquire new insights into their current mathematical understanding, so that they would be more likely to apply it successfully on future occasions. Examples of this approach include Barbara's discussion of the uses to which mathematics might be put (Chapter 4, pp. 61–3), Diane's lesson on the symbolism of a standard 'sum' (Chapter 4, pp. 65–70) and Laurie's development of the children's help boxes (Chapter 5, pp. 87–92). The success of such activities should be judged not so much on whether they were carried out as intended in the short term, but on whether they were likely to have a long-term impact on the way children approach mathematical problems in the future.

What kind of theories did the teachers have concerning application? As before, there was considerable diversity in the teachers' thinking, but nevertheless some common themes could be identified. In particular, several teachers emphasized that the activities they used should be *meaningful*, *relevant* or *motivating* for the children. No doubt this was partly because they wanted the children to engage with the activities, so that the objectives of the lesson would be achieved. But at the same time, the teachers often expressed the belief that raising the children's interest and motivation in an activity would play a positive role in increasing their readiness to apply mathematical knowledge. For example, Fiona justified her use of games in the following terms.

> I think playing a game together like that is a good motivating way to give . . . they see a reason for adding those numbers up. If I had said to them we were going to add those numbers together now, they would not have seen any point to it. They would probably have found it a lot more difficult.

One common way in which the teachers attempted to make activities meaningful and motivating was by *incorporating elements of 'real life'* in them. For example, children were at various times asked to imagine they were organizing a party, attending a car boot sale or painting the school shed. In some cases, the children were doing more than imagining, such as when Kathy asked her children to design some shelving for the classroom. Each of these activities allowed mathematical calculations – which typically involved money or measurement – to be embedded within a 'real-world' context. At the same time, the teachers believed that the 'real-life' nature of the activities would provide the rationale or motivation necessary for successful application.

Another way in which the teachers attempted to develop connections between children's mathematics and 'real life' was through the *use of story*. Both Barbara and Diane asked children to devise number stories that illustrated particular additions or subtractions, while Laurie asked his class to write stories in which particular mathematical operations were embedded. The main justification offered for these activities was that they would help children see the 'relevance' or 'use' to which mathematics could be put. The assumption was that if children were able to construct imaginary situations in which mathematics might be used, then they would be more likely to apply their knowledge when they encountered a mathematical problem located in a real situation.

The teachers' approaches and theories of learning

How did the approaches to application taken by the project teachers compare with the three theoretical perspectives described in Chapter 1? At first sight, it would seem that the teachers' approaches do not fit neatly into any of these three perspectives: none of the teachers can be clearly identified as having an 'associationist', 'constructivist' or 'situated cognition' approach to application. At the same time, it is possible to identify elements of all three theoretical approaches in what the teachers were saying and doing.

At times, when the teachers designed activities for the children to use a particular mathematical operation, they appeared to be operating on associationist lines. That is, they appeared to assume that if the activities were sufficiently similar to ones in which the children had previously encountered that operation, then they would be more likely to use it again. The most explicit example of this was provided by Heather, who designed the 'Party time!' activity as an exercise in applying division. Heather was somewhat surprised when the children did not in fact use division to solve the problems, saying, 'I was hoping that they would say, "Ah, this is like the work we did the other day, when we had all those dividing sums to do, we just divide that, that and that and there we are." ' In other words, she had assumed that the children would make the necessary associations.

In the same way, it is possible to identify some elements of constructivist thinking in the teachers' own theorizing about application. These elements were most likely to appear when the teachers were reflecting on their own role in encouraging application. For example, we saw in Chapter 5 how Irene was concerned that her children should acquire a 'structure' (her term) that would enable them to 'order their thoughts' and thus facilitate application. However, she made it clear that she did not think it would be sufficient if the children simply followed a structure they had been given, saying, 'if they can make that structure for themselves, and adapt it as they go along, then that is application'. It is also a clear account of learning from a constructivist position.

At first sight, there might appear to be connections between the teachers' approaches to application and the perspective of situated cognition. As we saw earlier, theorists working within this perspective have suggested that learners should be introduced to 'authentic' experiences of the subject they are attempting to master. Thus students should learn mathematics, as far as it is possible, through being an apprentice mathematician meeting problems in the ways in which mathematicians might encounter them. At the start of the project, the idea of 'authentic activities' was discussed with the teachers, and several used this term when talking about their approach to application. However, the teachers' understanding of the term appeared to be different from that intended by theory. Rather than seeking to introduce activities that were authentic to the practice of mathematics, they tried instead to introduce activities that were authentic to other practices, both inside and outside the school. Thus Kathy considered she was using 'authentic activities' when she asked the children to order some school shelving, while Alice also considered the car boot sale to be an 'authentic activity'. In the teachers' search for activities that might be considered 'authentic', the question 'authentic to what?' tended not to get asked.

Conceptualizing application in Japan

A rather different perspective on application was provided by our visit to Japan. As we saw in Chapter 6, the Japanese teachers whom we interviewed did not see application as a problem. They also made no explicit attempt to teach for application in their lessons. In this respect, they were no doubt reflecting the lack of attention given to application within the Japanese national curriculum. At the same time, their practice suggested they were providing plenty of opportunities for children to apply their mathematical knowledge to a range of practical problems. In addition, the emphasis placed on communication between pupils in a whole class setting meant that Japanese children were having to explain their own thinking – and in some cases, other children's thinking – on a daily basis. The implicit theory of learning underlying this approach could well be summed up by paraphrasing the old Nuffield dictum of 'I do and I understand'. In the Japanese case, it seemed to be 'I explain and I understand'.

Implementing the National Numeracy Strategy

The teaching of mathematics in English primary schools is currently dominated by the National Numeracy Strategy. As we saw in Chapter 2, the strategy lays down the broad objectives for raising standards of numeracy, while the Numeracy Framework provides the details of what is to be taught and how it should be taught. Primary teachers now have very specific curricular objectives, which place much greater emphasis than before on oral and mental mathematics. They are also expected to conduct a daily mathematics lesson, involving the whole class in high levels of communication about mathematics.

What priority will be given to application as the National Numeracy Strategy is implemented in schools? At present, it is hard to know how things will unfold. As we saw in Chapter 2, teachers are receiving mixed messages on this issue. Both the strategy and the Numeracy Framework use a broad definition of numeracy, which includes *'an inclination and ability to solve number problems in a variety of contexts'* (DfEE 1999, section 1: 4) and the Framework itself contains an explicit strand on 'solving problems'. However, a closer inspection of the 'key objectives' and recommended examples provided by the Numeracy Framework suggests that the priority is very much on calculation skills and number knowledge at the expense of application.

There is a real concern, then, that as the National Numeracy Strategy is implemented in schools, teachers will give priority to teaching the skills of numeracy and relatively little attention to teaching the application of these skills. We would argue that such a narrow interpretation of numeracy should be resisted. Those centrally involved in implementing the strategy – such as numeracy consultants and 'leading mathematics teachers' – have a key role to play in keeping application in the foreground. There is no point in teaching pupils to be 'numerate' if they cannot apply what they know.

One way in which teachers can give priority to application is by making sure that the objectives in the 'solving problems' strand of the Numeracy Framework are fully addressed. In the course of this book, we have described a wide range of activities – from both Key Stages 1 and 2 – and indicated how they might be used to meet the objectives of this strand. As we have made clear, these examples are not intended as 'models of good practice' that should be copied unthinkingly. Rather, they are intended as starting points that teachers might use in developing their own practice. At the same time, we would suggest that some of the activities described in Chapters 3, 4 and 5 have at least as much potential (if not more) for promoting application compared with some of the examples that accompany the Numeracy Framework.

Teaching for application: issues and dilemmas

Teaching for application is not easy. There are no instant solutions or right answers. We do not know for sure whether the approaches described here will be more or less successful than other approaches. We do know, however, that they raise a number of issues and dilemmas that need to be addressed whenever teachers are planning to teach for application.

Practice or application?

In some of the activities described in Chapters 4 and 5, the teachers were hoping that the children would use a particular number operation; usually one that they had recently been using in the classroom. In the car boot sale, for example, Alice wanted the children to use subtraction, while in 'Party time!' Heather wanted the children use division. These examples raise the question of whether they are merely exercises in the 'practice' of particular skills, or whether they do in fact provide genuine opportunities for 'application'.

Clearly, the distinction between practice and application is not an easy one to make. Indeed, it might be more helpful to think in terms of the concepts of 'near' and 'far' transfer that we introduced in Chapter 1 (see p. 6). These concepts refer to the degree of similarity between the contexts in which a concept is learned and the one in which it is used. If the context are similar, then they are said to require 'near transfer'. When they are quite different, they are said to require 'far transfer'.

One advantage of this distinction is that it suggests a continuum along which particular examples of application can be located. The implication is that, when teaching for application, teachers need to consider ways in which the 'application context' differs from the 'teaching context'. While it is relatively easy for teachers to design tasks where the two contexts are very similar, they may only be promoting 'near transfer', or the practice of routine calculation skills. Conversely, if they want to encourage genuine application, or 'far transfer', they may need to design tasks that are quite novel for the children, and that involve them in analysing the nature of the problem, selecting from a range of possible strategies, monitoring their progress and providing a coherent explanation of what they have done.

'Real life' in the classroom?

The Numeracy Framework stresses that pupils should encounter 'real-life' problems, particularly if these involve money or measures. But any attempt to introduce 'real-life' activities into a classroom has to confront a fundamental dilemma. However hard the teacher may try to disguise it, the supposedly 'real-life' activity remains essentially a classroom activity. In other words, it is shaped by factors such as the teacher's curricular objectives, by the resources and materials that she makes available, by her need to manage the behaviour of a class of pupils, and, perhaps crucially, by the children's perceptions that they are carrying out a classroom activity and not engaging with real life. As a result, there will inevitably be a tension within the activity between its 'real-life' and its classroom features; a tension that may hinder rather than help the activity's intended functions.

We saw several examples of this tension operating earlier in this book. There were occasions when the teacher's curricular objectives meant that the pupils were not allowed to use certain resources that in real life would have been quite acceptable. For example, when Kathy set up an intended 'authentic' activity, in which her pupils calculated the VAT on the school shelving, she did not allow them to use the calculator in working out their answer. Yet in real life, calculators are often used in the calculation of VAT. As a result, Kathy's decision deprived the activity of an important aspect of its 'authenticity'.

On other occasions, the children responded to an activity by using mathematical strategies which would have been quite acceptable in real life, but which conflicted with the teachers' curricular objectives. For example, when Heather set up the 'Party time!' activity, she intended her children to solve the problems by using their recently acquired knowledge of division. Instead, the pupils solved the problems by using methods – such as successive multiplication and estimation – that might well have been used by people organizing parties in real life.

There is no obvious way out of this dilemma. Nevertheless, as with the issue of practice or application, it may be helpful for teachers to think in terms of a continuum. At one extreme, there are activities that are basically classroom exercises, and where the 'real-life' content is minimal. Many standard 'word problems', including some of the examples recommended in the Numeracy Framework, fit clearly into this category. At the other extreme are activities that are firmly rooted in real life, and where the constraints of the classroom have been reduced as far as possible. In practice, activities at this end of the continuum are likely to be much messier and harder for the teacher to control: however, they may have greater value in promoting application.

The role of the teacher

One issue that occurred repeatedly during our project concerned the role that the teachers should play in promoting application. During project meetings, there was considerable discussion about the extent to which the teachers should intervene in the learning process and about the kinds of intervention that might be most effective. Not only were there different perspectives within the group, but there were also conflicts within the teachers themselves. There were contradictions in their beliefs about how and when to intervene, or discrepancies between what they believed and how they behaved in practice.

A good example of such conflicts was provided by Alice in Chapter 4. Before the car boot sale, Alice said that she was 'not sure that application takes place when under the control of the teacher'. Later, however, she said, 'I think adult intervention is quite important. Children need to be shown certain strategies . . . or have a model.' Her own behaviour during the car boot sale reflected this conflict over her role. For example, she gave children explicit practice before the sale in the methods they were to use, and during the sale itself she explicitly modelled the process of giving change. At the same time, she encouraged the children to develop their own methods for keeping track of money.

Clearly, there are advantages and disadvantages to both intervention and non-intervention. The advantage of non-intervention is that it may give the children time and space to decide on their own approach to a problem or to discuss possible approaches with other children. The disadvantage is that it may be hard to identify or sort out misconceptions or misunderstandings. Similarly, the advantage of intervention is that, if done sensitively and according to a clear plan, it can help the children develop their thinking: a good example of this was provided by Irene in Chapter 5 (pp. 80–1). On the other hand, intervention may direct children down particular avenues that are neither intended nor beneficial. For example, when Claire provided a model for her class of a particular combination of colours in the winter picture activity (Chapter 3, pp. 41–3), she was surprised to find that almost all the class reproduced the same combination of colours as she had used in her model. In this case, the children simply interpreted their task as copying what the teacher had done.

Children explaining their reasoning

Successive versions of the National Curriculum made it clear that children should be given opportunities to *'explain their reasoning'* as part of 'Using and Applying Mathematics'. Similarly, the Numeracy Framework makes it clear that children should be able to *'explain methods and reasoning about numbers orally and in writing'* (DfEE 1999, section 6: 76). Over the years this requirement has caused teachers considerable difficulty, and the teachers on our project were no exception in this respect.

Some of the teachers appeared to give little attention to children explaining their reasoning. They set up activities for pupils to work through on their own, or made few demands on pupils to talk about what they were doing. Other teachers tried various approaches to get pupils to explain their thought processes to them, although none found it particularly easy. Irene, for example, asked her children to talk through how they would solve a problem before they actually embarked on it, with somewhat mixed results. Kathy, in contrast, allowed the children to work on the VAT problem on their own, and then asked them to explain to her how they had arrived at their estimate; as we saw, this caused them considerable difficulty. Fiona, too, found it difficult to get her pupils to discuss their thinking with her, commenting that, 'They find that very difficult. They do not know what they have done themselves . . . You don't know how to get them to say without putting words in their mouths.'

Other teachers approached the problem in a different way. Instead of asking children to explain their thinking to the teacher, they tried to get the children to work in groups and explain their thinking to each other. Perhaps the clearest example of this was provided by Claire, who provided the two case studies in Chapter 3. At a later stage in the project, Claire devised an activity in which the children were asked to generate number sentences on 'breakthrough' cards. They then had to justify the correctness of these sentences to the other children by using cars and a model roundabout. As Claire said, 'It's a good way of really knowing if they understand, talking each other through their mistakes, each child talking them through the mistakes. I think it is less threatening than a teacher wanting to talk through mistakes.'

Our observations in Japan suggest that this might be an area where teachers in England and Wales could learn from approaches used elsewhere. In virtually every lesson we observed, children were expected to discuss their methods and explain their thinking to the teacher and to each other. The Japanese children seemed to be quite comfortable with this practice, and showed few inhibitions about exposing errors and incomplete understandings to their peers. It was clearly something they had encountered on a daily basis since their first days in primary school.

Children applying 'real-life' knowledge in the classroom

Our main concern in this book has been with the ways in which children can apply the mathematical knowledge gained in school to a range of novel contexts. Yet we should not forget that children also have a range of knowledge – including some ideas about mathematics – that has been developed or acquired outside the classroom. If we are to help children apply their knowledge, we need to look for ways in which this knowledge can be used inside school. Of course, a full discussion of this topic is well beyond the scope of this book. Our intention here is merely to raise the issue, and to provide some examples from the project of children bringing – or not bringing – their real-world knowledge into the classroom.

One way in which children may use this kind of knowledge is to check whether the answer they have obtained to a problem is reasonable. This happened most noticeably during the 'Party time!' activity, when Ceri and Marilyn rejected an answer of 224 packets of biscuits. They reasoned, quite realistically, that '£2.50 is not the sort of money that you could buy 224 packets of biscuits with'. On other occasions, however, children obtained an unrealistic solution to a problem, but were still prepared to accept it. The most noticeable example of this occurred during the PE shed problem (see Chapter 5, pp. 79–84). Here Suzanne was quite happy with her answer that 500 pots of paint were needed to paint the school PE shed. In this case, we do not know whether Suzanne lacked the appropriate real-world knowledge, or whether she simply failed to apply it. It seems likely, however, that her main experience of pots of paint may have been of the small pots that she used in the classroom or at home. From this perspective, it might not be at all unreasonable to think that 500 pots would be needed to paint the PE shed.

We also observed an occasion where the pupils obtained a correct answer to a problem, but rejected it on the grounds that it did not fit with their own 'real-world' experience. This occurred during the help boxes activity (see Chapter 5, p. 89) when Laurie's pupils were trying to work out how much space was available to each player on a football pitch. Here, the pupils correctly worked out that the answer was 366 square yards, but they rejected it as it did not equate with their actual experience of playing football. Ironically, the children here applied their real-world knowledge in order to 'check whether their result was reasonable', but as a result they failed to solve the problem correctly.

Beyond numeracy?

We conclude by restating our main theme. Children attend school in order to acquire knowledge that will be useful to them in the rest of their lives. This is as true for mathematics as it is for any other area of the curriculum. We want pupils to be numerate, not so they can carry out feats of mental arithmetic in school, but so they can confidently apply their knowledge of mathematics to a range of situations in their subsequent working and domestic lives. There is no point in teaching pupils to be 'numerate' if they cannot apply what they know.

Stating the problem is easy. Addressing it, as we have seen, is much harder. We have tried in this book to provide different ways of looking at the problem, to describe possible teaching approaches and to raise some of the theoretical and practical issues involved. We hope that teachers, curriculum designers and researchers will take up our challenge to keep application high on their respective agendas, and to continue the search for solutions that work both in theory and in practice.

References

Adams, M.J. (1990) *Beginning to Read: Thinking and Learning about Print*. Cambridge, MA: MIT Press.

Askew, M. (1996) 'Using and Applying Mathematics' in schools: reading the texts, in D.C. Johnson and A. Millett (eds) *Implementing the Mathematics National Curriculum: Policy, Politics and Practice*. London: Paul Chapman.

Askew, M., Brown, M., Johnson, D.C. *et al.* (1993) *Evaluation of the Implementation of National Curriculum Mathematics at Key Stages 1, 2 and 3*. London: School Curriculum and Assessment Authority.

Brown, G. (1995) What is involved in learning?, in C.W. Desforges (ed.) *An Introduction to Teaching*. Oxford: Blackwell Publishers Ltd.

Brown, M. (1996) The context of the research – the evolution of the National Curriculum for mathematics, in D.C. Johnson and A. Millett (eds) *Implementing the Mathematics National Curriculum: Policy, Politics and Practice*. London: Paul Chapman.

Brown, M., Askew, M., Baker, D., Denvir, H. and Millett, A. (1998) Is the National Numeracy Strategy research-based?, *British Journal of Educational Studies*, 46(4): 362–85.

Brown, J.S., Collins, A. and Duguid, P. (1989) Situated cognition and the culture of learning, *Educational Researcher*, 18(1): 32–42.

Cockcroft, W.H. (1982) *Mathematics Counts: Report of the Committee of Inquiry into the Teaching of Mathematics in Schools*. London: HMSO.

Department for Education (DfE) (1995) *Mathematics in the National Curriculum*. London: HMSO.

Department for Education and Employment (DfEE) (1998a) *Numeracy Matters: The Preliminary Report of the Numeracy Task Force*. London: DfEE.

Department for Education and Employment (DfEE) (1998b) *The Implementation of the National Numeracy Strategy: The Final Report of the Numeracy Task Force*. London: DfEE.

Department for Education and Employment (DfEE) (1999) *The National Numeracy*

Strategy: Framework for Teaching Mathematics from Reception to Year 6. London: DfEE.

Department of Education and Science (DES) (1977) *Curriculum 11–16: Working Papers by HMI.* London: HMSO.

Department of Education and Science (DES) (1979) *Mathematics 5–11: A Handbook of Suggestions.* London: HMSO.

Department of Education and Science (DES) (1985) *Better Schools.* London: HMSO.

Department of Education and Science (DES) (1989a) *Mathematics in the National Curriculum.* London: HMSO.

Department of Education and Science (DES) (1989b) *Mathematics in the National Curriculum: Non-Statutory Guidance.* London: HMSO.

Department of Education and Science (DES) (1991) *Mathematics in the National Curriculum.* London: HMSO.

Harris, S., Keys, W. and Fernandes, C. (1997) *Third International Mathematics and Science Study, Second National Report, Part 1.* Slough: National Foundation for Educational Research (NFER).

Her Majesty's Inspectorate (HMI) (1991) *Mathematics Key Stages 1 and 3: A Report by HM Inspectorate on the First Year 1989–1990.* London: HMSO.

Johnson, D.C and Millett, A. (1996) The research programme 1991–3: Data, data analyses and selected results, in D.C. Johnson and A. Millett (eds) *Implementing the Mathematics National Curriculum: Policy, Politics and Practice.* London: Paul Chapman.

National Assessment of Educational Progress (NAEP) (1983) *The Third National Mathematics Assessment.* Denver, CO: Education Commission of the States.

National Curriculum Council (NCC) (1992) *Using and Applying Mathematics: Books A and B.* York: NCC.

Nunes, T., Schliemann, A. and Carraher, D. (1993) *Street Mathematics and School Mathematics.* Cambridge: Cambridge University Press.

Piaget, J. (1952) *The Child's Conception of Number.* London: Routledge and Kegan Paul.

Piaget, J. (1972) *The Principles of Genetic Epistemology.* London: Routledge and Kegan Paul.

Piaget, J. and Inhelder, B. (1966) *The Psychology of the Child.* London: Routledge and Kegan Paul.

Reynolds, D. and Farrell, S. (1996) *Worlds Apart? A Review of International Surveys of Educational Achievement involving England.* London: HMSO.

Säljö, R. and Wyndhamn, J. (1990) Problem-solving, academic performance and situated reasoning: a study of joint cognitive activity in the formal setting, *British Journal of Educational Psychology,* 60(3): 245–54.

Singley, M.K. and Anderson, J.R. (1989) *Transfer of Cognitive Skill.* Cambridge, MA: Harvard University Press.

Thorndike, E.L. (1913) *The Psychology of Learning.* New York: Teachers College Press.

Index

ISSUES IN TEACHING NUMERACY IN PRIMARY SCHOOLS

Ian Thompson (ed.)

This timely book provides a detailed and comprehensive overview of the teaching and learning of numeracy in primary schools. It will be particularly helpful to teachers, mathematics co-ordinators and numeracy consultants involved in the implementation of the National Numeracy Strategy. It presents an accessible guide to current British and Dutch research into numeracy teaching. Leading researchers describe their findings and discuss implications for practising teachers. The projects include studies of effective teachers of numeracy and ICT and numeracy, an evaluation of international primary textbooks, assessment, using and applying mathematics, and family numeracy. The book also includes chapters on pedagogy, focusing on the teaching of mental calculation; the transition from mental to written algorithms; the place of the empty number line; and the use of the calculator as a teaching aid. Most chapters include practical suggestions for helping teachers develop aspects of their numeracy teaching skill.

Contents

224pp   0 335 20324 8 (Paperback)   0 335 20325 6 (Hardback)

ENRICHING EARLY MATHEMATICAL LEARNING

Grace Cook, Lesley Jones, Cathy Murphy and Gillian Thumpston

This book is a rich resource intended to support practising and trainee teachers with their teaching of mathematics in the early years. It comprises twenty activities which can be used as starting points. For each activity there are suggestions about how children might respond and guidance as to how the children may be further developed as learners. Support is also given to enable the teacher to embed the learning in a theoretical framework and make links with the National Curriculum.

All of the activities have been tried and tested in school and suggestions are made about the way in which these might be integrated into general classroom topics. There is a strong focus on formative assessment and how this can inform future planning.

Special features include:

- very accessible to teachers
- attractive and user-friendly format
- detailed support for introducing and extending activities which cover each area of the National Curriculum
- focus on using and applying maths at the early stages of Key Stage 1.

Contents

Introduction – Activities linked to the National Curriculum Programmes of Study – Handfuls – Ladybirds – Rosie the hen – Jumps and hops – Number ladder – Calculator numbers – HIgher and lower – Secret number – Feely bag pairs – Boxes – Comparing containers – Towers – Robots – Wrapping paper – Here comes the dustcart – Dolly mixtures – Fabric beanies – What's missing? – Egg boxes – Unifix towers – Appendix – Resources – Bibliography.

104pp   0 335 19666 7 (Paperback)